Enameled Kitchenware

American & European

David T. Pikul &
Ellen M. Plante

4880 Lower Valley Road, Atglen, PA 19310 USA

Front Cover:
A beautiful German three-cup laundry set for soap, sand, etc., white with an unusual, decorative floral ribbon/motif. *Courtesy of David T. Pikul, The Chuctanunda Antique Co.* $500- 600.

Back Cover:
Even the canine companion can enjoy enameled ware. Here Pudgie contemplates his enameled dog dish. *Courtesy of David T. Pikul, The Chuctanunda Antique Co.* $125-175.

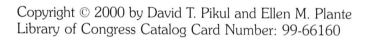

Copyright © 2000 by David T. Pikul and Ellen M. Plante
Library of Congress Catalog Card Number: 99-66160

ISBN: 0-7643-1022-4

Book Design by Anne Davidsen
Typeset in Benguiat Bk BT/Souvenir Lt BT

Printed in China
1 2 3 4

Published by Schiffer Publishing Ltd.
4880 Lower Valley Road
Atglen, PA 19310
Phone: (610) 593-1777; Fax: (610) 593-2002
e-mail: schifferbk@aol.com
Please visit our website catalog at
www.schifferbooks.com
or write for a free printed catalog.
This book may be purchased from the publisher.
Please include $3.95 for shipping.

In Europe, Schiffer books are distributed by
Bushwood Books
6 Marksbury Avenue
Kew Gardens
Surrey TW9 4JF England
Phone: 44 (0)208 392-8585;
Fax: 44 (0)208 392-9876
e-mail: bushwd@aol.com

Please try your bookstore first.

We are interested in hearing from authors
with book ideas on related subjects.

Contents

Dedication & Acknowledgment

For that adventurous spirit - the enameled ware collector and with special thanks to Peter Schiffer, Jennifer Lindbeck, and Brandi Wright our editor at Schiffer Publishing, Ltd. We would also like to extend a very special thank you to Tom Pikul and Daniel Bertrand for their research and translation efforts. Sincere thanks also go to Ted Plante and to Sarah Pikul for the beautiful photographs she shot in France and a warm "we couldn't have done it without you" thanks to Alton Vogle for his unending support and assistance with photographs. Last but far from least we would like to recognize the contribution made by Rick Jones and Pamela DeBisschop in allowing items from their collections to be included in this work and we would like to thank Tracie DeBisschop for providing her lovely home as a backdrop for several photographs. All photographs by David Pikul unless otherwise indicated.

Large European coffee biggin, 14" tall, double handles, rare pink with cherry design. *Courtesy of David T. Pikul, The Chuctanunda Antique Co.* $375-450. Photo by Sarah Pikul.

European sugar bowl with a decorative bird design. *Courtesy of David T. Pikul, The Chuctanunda Antique Co.* $300-400. Photo by Sarah Pikul.

Foreword

After the publication of *Collectible Enameled Ware: American & European* in January 1998, the feedback we received most frequently from collectors, book reviewers, antiques dealers, and interior designers concerned their surprise, amazement, and delight at the myriad, beautiful graphic designs adorning collectible enameled ware. With this in mind, *Enameled Kitchen Ware: American & European* is a continuing celebration and visual tour of the wide variety of circa late 1800s - 1940 enameled household objects available for collecting today. This work endeavors to illustrate unusual or striking pieces as well as more familiar examples of American and European enameled objects intended to outfit the kitchens (and other rooms of the home) before glass, aluminum, and plastic came on the scene and moved enameled ware into temporary obscurity.

Readers will note that each photo caption includes a value range. Values are determined by age, condition, object, color, decoration, and rarity. Values can also be determined by the country or region of a particular country where the object is sold. Therefore, the authors assume no responsibility in this regard but strongly encourage you to purchase the best you can afford from dealers specializing in this area and invest in those enameled ware pieces that bring you pleasure or add a decorative element to your home or place of business. Whether it's the nostalgia factor, decorative potential, or the aesthetic beauty of an object that fuels your collecting passion, there are new enameled ware treasures constantly turning up - an unusual shade of color, a different pattern, an eye-catching graphic design - and we are pleased to be able to offer you a glimpse of what awaits.

A French footbath with handles, 13" wide, blue with a floral/bird motif. *Courtesy of Pam DeBisschop.* $400-500.

Introduction

An Overview of Enameled Ware

Enameling as an art form was developed by ancient civilizations but it became an industry targeting utilitarian household goods during the nineteenth century after several decades of experimentation. Germany, long prolific in the production of enameled ware, was among the first of the European countries to achieve success in applying the glass-like finish to everyday objects made of iron and then later, sheet-steel. Belgium, too, was an important center of enameled ware production and the town of Gosselies became an ideal site for several such factories during the mid-nineteenth century due to its abundance of natural resources. One factory in particular, founded by a German named David Moll, did in fact produce some of the most beautiful and exceptional pieces of enameled ware (circa 1850s and 1860s). Some of his work, including two magnificent jardinières, was displayed at the 1860 World's Fair held in St. Louis, Missouri.

The manufacture of enameled ware was a multi-step process involving machinery as well as skilled, hands-on work. The talents of those working with cast-iron or sheet steel are certainly not to be underestimated. A careful balance regarding the chemical and physical properties of either metal had to be achieved in order for the enamel coating to adhere properly. Thanks to the development of the 1858 Bessemer process and continued advances in metalwork during the 1860s, production of enameled goods made with sheet steel was well under way. It's interesting to note, however, the first objects targeted for household use were cast-iron pots enameled on the inside only. From there we see the progression to sheet steel and the entire pot or kettle being coated with enamel.

In producing enameled ware the metal had to first be cut by hand to the desired size or was cut in strips and edges rounded to fashion a smooth finish. Mechanical presses (often operated by women) were not available or in widespread use until the 1890s, therefore a gifted metalworker was paid handsomely for his skill. During the nineteenth century this also meant handles (which early on were flat) and buttons or knobs were attached with rivets while during the early twentieth century they were welded to the particular object. (For collectors this can be a valuable way to help determine the approximate age of a piece.)

After the material was cut it had to be cleaned or properly prepared to accept the porcelain-enamel glaze or finish. Generally this involved polishing the metal to remove any traces of grease and then using an acid bath to remove chemical residue and impurities. Only then would the metal accept the ground coat of enamel. In the mean time, the lips had been cut on pitchers, rims curved, and the handles riveted or soldered. While these steps were being taken, the "frit" was being prepared.

The recipe for frit varied from one manufacturer to the next but included materials such as feldspar, sand, quartz, borax, and soda ash. To create a colored enamel glaze certain metallic oxides were added to the recipe. For example, a dark blue was achieved by including cobalt oxide, for green chromium oxide was added, and yellow meant mixing in sulfide of cadmium. The mixture was melted at a high degree of heat to achieve a molten glass that was then put in water where it separated into small particles. This mixture or frit was then transformed into a slip-glaze (a process called humid crushing) by mixing it with a certain percentage of water and clay and running it through a mill designed especially for that purpose.

Once this enamel making process was complete, assorted household items were treated to one or more coats of porcelain-enamel. This was done by hand or by machine depending upon whether the object was sprayed or dipped in a tank. Afterwards the items were fired in a kiln to bind the finish to the metal and then cooled slowly. Items were then inspected for irregularities or a sub-standard finish before any additional enamel coatings or decorations were applied. Despite the most stringent attention to detail, minor flaws such as air bubbles or crackles did occur from gases released during the initial firing. The number of rejected pieces was reportedly large enough to create a secondary industry in which smaller enameling firms concentrated their efforts on these less than perfect pieces, touching them up to sell.

The basic steps followed to create an enamel coating may have varied by degrees at the factories throughout Europe and the United States (indeed, it was often a highly guarded secret), but many of the finished products were similar in appearance if they were left plain or sported a marbled, mottled, or relish pattern. Where notable differences occur it is due to the objects themselves, colors, and the graphic designs or decorations used to adorn these humble household goods. For example, the lavabo, wall-hung utensil racks, coffee biggins, salt boxes, and canister sets were primarily produced and used throughout Europe. Old catalogs issued by German and French manufacturers indicate colors such as terra cotta, turquoise, and a marbled green and coral were popular abroad. And when it comes to graphic de-

This color illustration from an early twentieth century German catalog, *Saechsische Emaillir - und Stanzwerke*, depicts a coffee pot with a striking floral design. Note the item description is offered in several languages and the coffee pot is described as being welded. *Courtesy of Daniel Bertrand.*

This page from the same catalog offers a selection of wash basins with decorations based on Japanese designs. Birds and small flowers were especially popular on enameled ware produced during the late nineteenth century period. *Courtesy of Daniel Bertrand.*

signs, European firms made decorative design something akin to an art form whereas American manufacturers used them sparingly early on and then relied heavily on decals during the 1920s and 1930s.

By the last quarter of the nineteenth century numerous factories in Germany, France, Czechoslovakia, Austria, Poland, Belgium, Spain, Finland, Italy, Hungary, Norway, Sweden, Denmark, and Great Britain were turning out enameled ware targeted for the home. Many of these items were exported to the United States and sold along with the enameled goods produced by growing American firms. *Collectible Enameled Ware: American & European*, our first book on this subject, contains a select listing of manufacturers but it's worth noting here that those companies most prolific in the manufacture of enameled kitchen and household items included Annweiler, Nahrath Company, Baumann, and Bing Werke of Germany; Leopold & Company and Japy Freres & Company of France; Saint-Servais and Aubecq of Belgium; Riess Brothers of Austria; B.K. Emaile of The Netherlands; and Jacob J. Vollrath, Lalance and Grosjean, and the St. Louis Stamping Company of the United States.

Exactly what did these and hundreds of other smaller manufacturers produce? Kitchenware was a mainstay of the industry and common items included pots, kettles,

measuring pitchers, utensils, utensil racks, coffee pots, coffee biggins, cafetières (extremely large coffee dispensers taken by European men into the fields at harvest time), teapots, colanders, pie plates, fish kettles, cups and dishes, salt boxes, canisters, bread boxes, wall-hung towel racks, berry buckets, milk pails, muffin pans, syrup pitchers, milk pitchers, wall-hung containers for flour, potholders, and onions, match boxes, cake boxes, serving trays, trivets, roasting pans, and platters.

Others items used about the house include wall-hung towel/soap holders, candlesticks, gas irons, lavabos (a wall-hung "lavabo" or container which dispensed water for washing and a matching basin that was hung underneath to catch the water), wall-hung triple-cup laundry sets, wall-hung brush holders, tall (14 - 15") body pitchers used for bathing or fetching water from village wells, petrol cans, clocks, stacking dinner carriers, irrigators, water pitchers with matching basins (which were made in various sizes), covered chamber pails, decorative vases, ash trays, crumb trays, comb cases, kerosene lamps, umbrella stands, wall-hung soap dishes, and flasks.

A variety of other enameled items were produced including miniatures for the toy market (Germany, especially, produced a great deal of enameled toys for doll houses etc.), advertising give-aways and premiums, and

A third page from the catalog illustrates a toilette set with a matching water pitcher and basin, soap dish, toothbrush tray, and chamber pot. This is a wonderful example of enameled ware imitating more costly china and ceramics. *Courtesy of Daniel Bertrand.*

This same German catalog offered a variety of items including utilitarian buckets embellished with eye-catching floral designs. *Courtesy of Daniel Bertrand.*

personalized special orders that marked a particular celebration, anniversary, or notable event. Such one-of-a-kind objects are rare and therefore command a higher price in today's antiques market. Toys and advertising memorabilia have the distinction of being "cross collectibles" (for example, sought by the enameled ware collector and the toy collector) and as a result supply and demand impact pricing.

Enameled ware captured a lion's share of the household goods market between the late 1800s - 1940 period but advances in technology and new materials such as aluminum and glass oven-to-table bakeware took center stage by the early 1940s. Enameled ware was piled in the basement or attic, or moved to the garage as the new darlings of a modern age took over in the kitchen. Now, however, enameled ware (also called graniteware or agateware by collectors), which has been in the "collecting" spotlight for the past few decades, has seen a tremendous upsurge the past few years. Many collectors are drawn to a specific color or pattern while others build a collection around favorite objects or graphic designs. Condition of course is a primary factor in determining price but minimal damage such as small chips do not necessarily decrease the value of an otherwise presentable piece. An even greater degree of damage is acceptable for a rare or unusual piece and makes it no less

desirable. Collectors must keep in mind enameled ware was intended for everyday use so items in mint or perfect condition can be difficult to come by.

While we have focused on enameled ware produced between the late 1800s and about 1940, there are also enameled objects that were manufactured by foreign companies during the 1950s, 1960s, and 1970s. There is a definite market for these "collectibles" but be certain you can differentiate between earlier examples and these more modern items. In addition, and more recently, enameled ware is being reproduced in vintage forms and sold in the housewares department of specialty stores or through mail-order catalogues. Such reproductions are generally marked in some way (stamp, paper label) but a deliberate fake or forgery - newer enameled ware represented as old - is not. Knowledge is the best defense against a questionable purchase and seeking out those dealers that specialize in vintage enameled ware will help assure the authenticity and true value of your collection. Keep in mind enameled ware made during the late 1800s is likely to display seamed construction, riveted handles, flat handles, and/or hand painted decorations. After the turn of the century welding eventually replaced rivets and transfer prints or decals replaced decorations done entirely by hand (although many outlines or stencils were filled in or enhanced by hand).

Chapter One
Plain & Simple

Enameled ware produced in a singular color or a color with a contrasting rim, stripe, etc., may be plain and simple but is by no means drab or boring. Eye-catching, decorative collections have been built around vintage white enameled ware or colored pieces devoid of pattern or graphic design. In many instances, a plain and simple piece of enameled ware might be lettered to indicate contents. Canisters, bread boxes, salt boxes, match boxes, and triple-cup laundry sets are perfect examples. The script or block lettering that appears on many such items was achieved by hand painting, stencils, or decals.

Regarding color, much of the early European enameled ware and similar items produced in England were turned out in basic white just as the heavier ceramic goods of the same period were. Naturally there were advantages in marketing a new product when it had an appearance similar to household goods already considered tried and true. White was also associated with cleanliness and hygiene - an aspect that would see enameled ware produced extensively in white for hospital use in the United States during the 1920s and 1930s. These white pitchers, basins, and so on usually had blue or black edging designed to protect rims.

Color became an increasing important factor in production as enameled ware gained a stronghold in the housewares market. European firms were the first to experiment with the metallic oxides used to create color and popular period designs as well as the abundance of colors seen in the rural countryside often inspired a wide range of hues. In contrast, manufacturers in the United States looked to the growing focus on cheerful and bright kitchens to inspire their line of colors - everything from "bisque" and "emerald" to "Robin's egg blue." Cream enameled ware with green trim was especially popular during the 1920s and 1930s. In England, white and pastels such as soft blue and creamy yellow were the colors that predominated the enameled ware market. By the period 1930 - 1940, many European firms were producing a variety of colored enameled ware devoid of any decoration or adornment to coincide with the modern movement and as cost-effective measure. Collectors should also note that during this decade European factories routinely stamped their goods with a company mark or logo - something that was only done sporadically during the late 1800s and early 1900s.

A variation on solid-colored enameled ware are those pieces that display shading. There are many beautiful

Large French candlestick, plain white, and a personalized mug. *Courtesy of Pam DeBisschop.* Candlestick $150-175 and mug $150-175.

items that feature light and dark tones of a specific color that were created with a spray gun and a mechanized, rotating surface.

Along with white, plain and simple enameled ware is found in cream, pink, red, blue, yellow, brown, cobalt, etc. The majority of these pieces were produced during the late 1800s or during the 1930s - the in-between years given over to decorative patterns or items with graphic designs.

French wall-hung match box, 7" tall, pink with French lettering. *Courtesy of David T. Pikul, The Chuctanunda Antique Co.* $150-175.

European coffee biggin, 10" tall, white with blue bands. *Courtesy of David T. Pikul, The Chuctanunda Antique Co.* $200-250.

European body pitcher with hinged lid, 13" tall, white. *Courtesy of David T. Pikul, The Chuctanunda Antique Co.* $150-200.

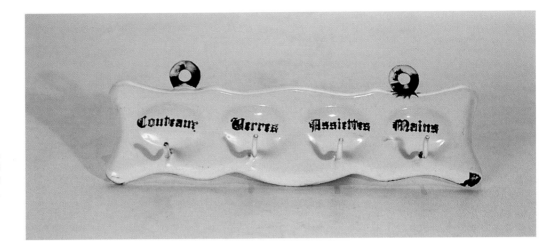

French wall-hung towel rack, rare small size, 7" long, white with black lettering. *Courtesy of Pam DeBisschop.* $200-250.

European candlesticks, each with a scalloped base, one white with pale green shading and the other blue. *Courtesy of David T. Pikul, The Chuctanunda Antique Co.* $40-50 each.

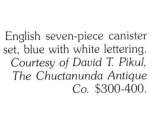

English seven-piece canister set, blue with white lettering. *Courtesy of David T. Pikul, The Chuctanunda Antique Co.* $300-400.

11

American wall-hung soap/toothbrush holder, white, rare piece. *Courtesy of David T. Pikul, The Chuctanunda Antique Co.* $125-150.

European coffee biggin, 10" tall, robin's egg blue with gilt trim. *Courtesy of David T. Pikul, The Chuctanunda Antique Co.* $175-200.

French wall-hung salt box with wooden lid, 10" tall, white with black lettering. *Courtesy of David T. Pikul, The Chuctanunda Antique Co.* $150-175.

English bread box, white with black handles and lettering. *Courtesy of David T. Pikul, The Chuctanunda Antique Co.* $150-175.

European coffee biggin, 10" tall, red with white bands. *Courtesy of David T. Pikul, The Chuctanunda Antique Co.* $250-300.

French wall-hung onion keeper, white with perforations and black lettering. *Courtesy of Pam DeBisschop.* $250-300.

European coffee biggin, 10 1/2" tall, white with red bands/rim. *Courtesy of David T. Pikul, The Chuctanunda Antique Co.* $175-200.

European lunch bucket, 9" tall, white with brown shading. *Courtesy of David T. Pikul, The Chuctanunda Antique Co.* $75-125.

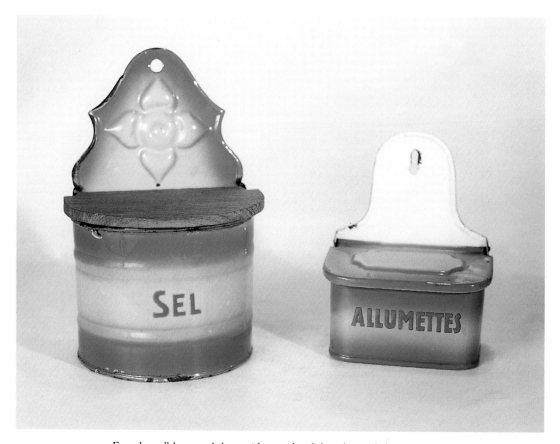

French wall-hung salt box with wooden lid and match box, blue shading and lettering. *Courtesy of David T. Pikul, The Chuctanunda Antique Co.* $175-225 each.

French six-piece canister set, graduating sizes, white with blue bands and lettering. *Courtesy of David T. Pikul, The Chuctanunda Antique Co.* $400-500.

French inhaler, blue with black lettering. *Courtesy of David T. Pikul, The Chuctanunda Antique Co.* $175-250. Photo by Sarah Pikul.

German wall-hung flour box with wooden lid, 10" tall, black lettering. *Courtesy of David T. Pikul, The Chuctanunda Antique Co.* $250-300.

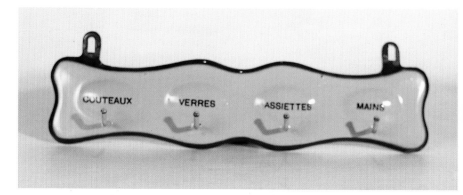

French wall-hung salt box, 10" tall, red with white lettering. *Courtesy of David T. Pikul, The Chuctanunda Antique Co.* $175-225.

French wall-hung towel rack, 12" long, yellow with brown lettering and trim. *Courtesy of David T. Pikul, The Chuctanunda Antique Co.* $150-175.

French three-cup laundry set, 15" wide, white with black trim and lettering. *Courtesy of David T. Pikul, The Chuctanunda Antique Co.* $150-175.

16

French six-piece canister set, graduating sizes, blue with white lettering and metal lids. *Courtesy of David T. Pikul, The Chuctanunda Antique Co.* $300-400.

European wall-hung soap dish, white. *Courtesy of David T. Pikul, The Chuctanunda Antique Co.* $95-125.

Large French coffee biggin, 14" tall, white with gilt trim and green/yellow bands. *Courtesy of David T. Pikul, The Chuctanunda Antique Co.* $275-350. Photo by Sarah Pikul.

Three European containers with lids, largest is 5" tall, blue. *Courtesy of David T. Pikul, The Chuctanunda Antique Co.* $50-75 each.

English flour container, 10" tall, white with black rim and lettering. *Courtesy of David T. Pikul, The Chuctanunda Antique Co.* $125-150.

French wall-hung salt box with lid, rare shape, blue with white lettering. *Courtesy of David T. Pikul, The Chuctanunda Antique Co.* $200-275.

American cocoa dipper, 14" long, white with a black rim. *Courtesy of David T. Pikul, The Chuctanunda Antique Co.* $100-150.

French pitcher, 5" tall, yellow. *Courtesy of David T. Pikul, The Chuctanunda Antique Co.* $50-75.

French butter dish with saucer and lid, white with gilt bands. *Courtesy of David T. Pikul, The Chuctanunda Antique Co.* $150-175.

American tea kettle, Art Deco styling, blue with metal trim. *Courtesy of David T. Pikul, The Chuctanunda Antique Co.* $150-175.

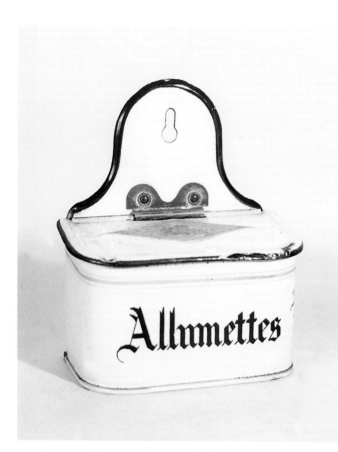

American shaving mug, white with metal base. *Courtesy of David T. Pikul, The Chuctanunda Antique Co.* $150-200.

French wall-hung match box, 7" tall, white with black trim and lettering. *Courtesy of David T. Pikul, The Chuctanunda Antique Co.* $150-175.

European coffee biggin, 10" tall, white with red trim/bands of color. *Courtesy of David T. Pikul, The Chuctanunda Antique Co.* $175-250.

American stove toaster, white with a black wooden handle. *Courtesy of David T. Pikul, The Chuctanunda Antique Co.* $150-200.

Fish boiler, white with green shading. *Courtesy of Pam DeBisschop.* $200-275.

European measuring pitcher, 9" tall, red with orange shading. *Courtesy of David T. Pikul, The Chuctanunda Antique Co.* $50-75.

European syrup pitcher with hinged lid, 6" tall, white with lavender shading and gilt trim. *Courtesy of David T. Pikul, The Chuctanunda Antique Co.* $175-200.

French coffee pot, 9" tall, white with gilt trim/bands. *Courtesy of David T. Pikul, The Chuctanunda Antique Co.* $175-250.

European coffee pot, 9" tall, white with light blue shading. *Courtesy of David T. Pikul, The Chuctanunda Antique Co.* $200-275.

French wall-hung salt box, 10" tall, white with medium blue shading and lettering. *Courtesy of David T. Pikul, The Chuctanunda Antique Co.* $250-275.

French six-piece canister set, graduating sizes, white bands and lettering. *Courtesy of David T. Pikul, The Chuctanunda Antique Co.* $500-600.

Large European coffee biggin, 13" tall, double handles, white with blue bands. *Courtesy of David T. Pikul, The Chuctanunda Antique Co.* $275-325.

French wall-hung match box, 7" tall, white with pale blue trim. *Courtesy of David T. Pikul, The Chuctanunda Antique Co.* $150-200.

American dipper, cream with a green rim and handle. *Courtesy of David T. Pikul, The Chuctanunda Antique Co.* $50-75.

European wall-hung salt box, 10" tall, white with a blue band and rare rear hanger. *Courtesy of David T. Pikul, The Chuctanunda Antique Co.* $250-300.

Salt box in previous photo with rare rear hanger depicted.

French wall-hung salt box, 10" tall, white with red bands and lettering. *Courtesy of David T. Pikul, The Chuctanunda Antique Co.* $200-225.

American syrup pitcher with hinged lid, white with a black handle and trim. *Courtesy of Rick Jones.* $175-200. Photo by James Armstrong.

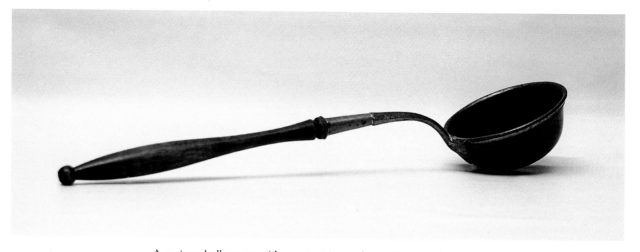

American ladle, gray with pewter trim and wooden handle.
Courtesy of Rick Jones. $200-300. Photo by James Armstrong.

Dutch canisters for sugar, tea, and coffee, yellow with metal lids and black lettering. *Courtesy of David T. Pikul, The Chuctanunda Antique Co.* $275-300.

European molds, different shades of blue. *Courtesy of David T. Pikul, The Chuctanunda Antique Co.* $150-200 each.

American coffee pot, "Bonnie Blue" by NESCO, white with blue coloring and a scalloped design. *Courtesy of Rick Jones.* $200-250. Photo by James Armstrong.

Chapter Two
Swirled, Marbled, Mottled, Feathered, Chicken Wire, & Snow on the Mountain

The words "swirl" and "marble" are often used interchangeably when describing enameled ware patterns but for the descriptive purposes of this book, swirled refers to a large pattern while marbled indicates a smaller pattern resembling the stone it's named after.

Decorative swirled and marbled patterns were achieved during the enameling process by hand dipping, machine dipping, or tong dipping an item (usually having a white base coat) into a secondary color. With hand dipping or tong dipping the factory worker was responsible for creating the pattern by turning the object and allowing the color to "run" until a desirable pattern was achieved. With machine dipping the high degrees of heat achieved during the firing process caused the white base coat to pass through the secondary color, resulting in a large swirled or small marbled pattern. Some factories relied on a special mix of "slip" to cause a marbling effect during firing.

In those instances where three or more colors are featured on an enameled object, collectors refer to this as "End of the Day." Many "End of the Day" items made in the United States sport a marbled pattern and value is significantly increased because of the additional color or colors. It is generally thought this was an expedient way of using left-over mixes toward the end of a production shift, hence the name. Then, too, because so much skill and hands-on work was required in the enameling process, it may simply have been a creative endeavor.

When it comes to swirled or marbled enameled ware, cobalt blue and white, old red and white, or "End of the Day" items are coveted by collectors. Swirled and marbled patterns were produced from the late 1800s through the 1930s but the older examples will demand a higher price. For example, when referring to the "old red" featured on enameled ware, it is a deeper, darker shade than the red found on circa 1930s enameled ware.

Swirled or marbled items are also found in color combinations such as gray and white, yellow and white, light or medium blue and white, aqua and white, pink and white, or black and white. These patterns often proved a cost-effective way for both American and European factories to turn out attractive goods during the early twentieth century. Today many collectors find striking collections can be built around these patterns.

Several other decorative patterns featured on enameled ware have acquired curious names given the fact that they resemble a sponged effect, a feather design, imitate a chicken wire pattern, or appear as a lumpy white design on a base coat of color which collectors refer to as "Snow on the Mountain."

Various production techniques were employed to create these patterns or the look was the result of firing in the kiln. Early on, when a great deal of the enameled ware produced in the United States was a mottled gray, a one-coat process known as selective etching allowed the pattern to form during firing. While this was a cost-effective means of production, the ongoing experiments with color and pattern led to more fanciful pieces having brighter colors and the two or three coats of enamel associated with quality.

Enameled objects with a speckled pattern were the result of a contrasting or secondary color simply being brush spattered on an item. Creating the lumpy "Snow on the Mountain" effect called for generous, thick amounts of white enamel to be applied over a colored base.

Chicken wire and feather patterns were the result of the various decorative/production processes used in creating enamel ware. Specific information on the development of these patterns has been difficult to uncover but chicken wire patterns may have been "printed" onto a base white coat with a roller and then fired while feathered patterns were achieved with a limited use of enamel slip and pearl ash to develop a subtle pattern during the firing process. Both are predominantly European patterns and as early as 1903 a German catalog advertised items with a chicken wire design. In this particular pattern, the majority of items found are blue and white (unless "End of the Day") but rare examples have been found with red, orange, and green coloring.

The value of mottled enameled ware is determined by color, object, and condition. This pattern is perhaps more common than the others mentioned above so it stands to reason that the value of enamel ware with chicken wire, feathered, speckled, or "Snow on the Mountain" increases accordingly.

American cream can with metal lid, "Columbian Ware,"
blue and white swirl. *Courtesy of Rick Jones.* $900-1000.
Photo by James Armstrong.

American syrup pitcher with metal lid, "Chrysolite" dark green
and white marbled pattern. *Courtesy of Rick Jones.* $1500-1800.
Photo by James Armstrong.

American coffee pot, 9 1/2" tall, blue and white marble with a black handle. *Courtesy of David T. Pikul, The Chuctanunda Antique Co.* $275-325.

French body pitcher, 15" tall, pink and white swirl. *Courtesy of David T. Pikul, The Chuctanunda Antique Co.* $350-425. Photo by Sarah Pikul.

French salt box with wooden lid, 10" tall, red and white "Snow on the Mountain" with black lettering. *Courtesy of David T. Pikul, The Chuctanunda Antique Co.* $300-400.

American chamber pot, "Columbian Ware," blue and white swirl with black handle. *Courtesy of Rick Jones.* $300-400. Photo by James Armstrong.

European coffee biggin, 11" tall, red and white marbled with red trim/handle/spout. *Courtesy of David T. Pikul, The Chuctanunda Antique Co.* $225-275.

European wall-hung irrigator, 9" tall, orange and black marbled. *Courtesy of David T. Pikul, The Chuctanunda Antique Co.* $250-300.

American coffee pot, 9" tall, brown and white swirl. *Courtesy of Rick Jones.* $600-700. Photo by James Armstrong.

American pitcher, 10" tall, "End of the Day" (three or more colors) marble pattern. *Courtesy of David T. Pikul, The Chuctanunda Antique Co.* $300-350.

American bowl, "Columbian Ware," cobalt blue and white swirl. *Courtesy of Rick Jones.* $300-400. Photo by James Armstrong.

American water pitcher and matching basin, "Columbian Ware,"
cobalt blue and white swirl. *Courtesy of Rick Jones.* $1200-1500.
Photo by James Armstrong.

American pan, 3 1/2" tall, blue and white swirl. *Courtesy of David T. Pikul, The Chuctanunda Antique Co.* $150-175.

American water pitcher, "Chrysolite," dark green and white marbled. *Courtesy of Rick Jones.* $400-500. Photo by James Armstrong.

European wall-hung soap/cloth dish, gray and white swirl. *Courtesy of David T. Pikul, The Chuctanunda Antique Co.* $250-300.

American rice ball, gray and white mottled. *Courtesy of Rick Jones.* $250-300. Photo by James Armstrong.

American chamber pail with lid and wooden handle, cobalt blue and white swirl. *Courtesy of Rick Jones.* $500-600. Photo by James Armstrong.

Three French candlesticks, a blue and white mottled, $125-150; center candlestick is green with a floral design, $150-200; and on the right is a blue and white swirl, $175-225. *Courtesy of Pam DeBisschop.*

American cuspidor, 14" diameter, light blue and white swirl. *Courtesy of David T. Pikul, The Chuctanunda Antique Co.* $300-400.

European coffee biggin, 10" tall, blue and white marbled with red trim. *Courtesy of David T. Pikul, The Chuctanunda Antique Co.* $275-350.

European footed trivet, 9" size, light blue and white swirl. *Courtesy of David T. Pikul, The Chuctanunda Antique Co.* $200-250.

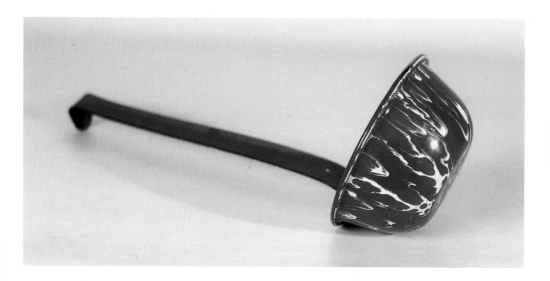

American dipper, red and white marbled with a solid red handle. *Courtesy of David T. Pikul, The Chuctanunda Antique Co.* $175-250.

American coffee pot, 11" tall, blue and white marbled. *Courtesy of David T. Pikul, The Chuctanunda Antique Co.* $300-400.

American child-size chamber pot with lid, "Columbian Ware," blue and white swirl with black handle. *Courtesy of Rick Jones.* $400-500. Photo by James Armstrong.

French wall-hung triple-soap for laundry, blue and white marbled with blue trim/lettering. *Courtesy of David T. Pikul, The Chuctanunda Antique Co.* $250-300.

European wall-hung utensil rack with two tools, 12" wide by 19" long, blue and white marbled. *Courtesy of David T. Pikul, The Chuctanunda Antique Co.* $250-300.

French salt box with wooden lid, 10" tall, blue and white marbled with blue lettering. *Courtesy of David T. Pikul, The Chuctanunda Antique Co.* $225-275.

European teapot with hinged lid, 4" tall, brown and white marbled. *Courtesy of David T. Pikul, The Chuctanunda Antique Co.* $350-400.

European chamber pail and matching body pitcher, blue and white swirl. *Courtesy of Pam DeBisschop.* $700-800 for the set.

American coffee pot, "Chrysolite" dark green and white swirl. *Courtesy of Rick Jones.* $600-700. Photo by James Armstrong.

European measuring pitcher, 9" tall, pink and white marbled. *Courtesy of David T. Pikul, The Chuctanunda Antique Co.* $225-275.

39

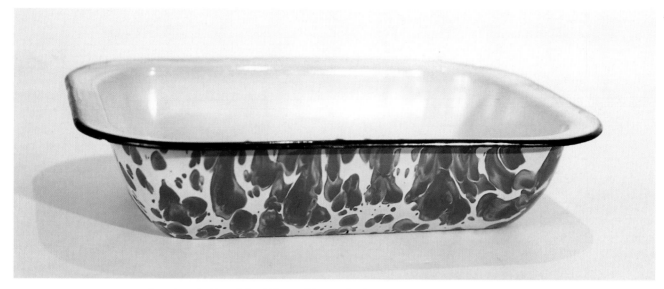

American baking dish, 10" size, blue and white swirl with black rim.
Courtesy of David T. Pikul, The Chuctanunda Antique Co. $150-200.

European kettle with lid, red and white mottled. *Courtesy of David T. Pikul, The Chuctanunda Antique Co.* $325-400.

American coffee pot, 10" tall, blue and white marbled with a black handle. *Courtesy of David T. Pikul, The Chuctanunda Antique Co.* $275-325.

American chamber pail with lid and wooden handle, blue and white marbled. *Courtesy of David T. Pikul, The Chuctanunda Antique Co.* $300-350.

European measuring pitcher, 9" tall, gray and white marbled. *Courtesy of David T. Pikul, The Chuctanunda Antique Co.* $225-275.

American tray, "End of the Day" coloring in a swirl pattern. *Courtesy of David T. Pikul, The Chuctanunda Antique Co.* $350-400.

French wall-hung salt box with wooden lid, 10" tall, blue and white marbled with blue lettering. *Courtesy of David T. Pikul, The Chuctanunda Antique Co.* $275-350.

Large American coffee boiler, iris and white marbled. *Courtesy of Rick Jones.* $400-500. Photo by James Armstrong.

American roaster with lid, cobalt blue and white swirl. *Courtesy of Rick Jones.* $500-600. Photo by James Armstrong.

American pan, 4" tall, blue and white swirl. *Courtesy of David T. Pikul, The Chuctanunda Antique Co.* $150-175.

European milk pail, 10" tall, red and white marbled with red rim. *Courtesy of David T. Pikul, The Chuctanunda Antique Co.* $275-300.

American water pitcher, cobalt blue and white swirl. *Courtesy of Rick Jones.* $600-700. Photo by James Armstrong.

European chamber pail with lid and wooden handle, 10" tall, light blue and white swirl. *Courtesy of David T. Pikul, The Chuctanunda Antique Co.* $250-325.

43

Three American cream cans, cobalt blue and white swirl. *Courtesy of Rick Jones.* $700- 800 each. Photo by James Armstrong.

American mixing bowl, "Columbian Ware," blue and white swirl. *Courtesy of Rick Jones.* $300-400. Photo by James Armstrong.

European coffee biggin, 10" tall, "End of the Day" pink, white, and green in a large mottled pattern. *Courtesy of David T. Pikul, The Chuctanunda Antique Co.* $500-600. Photo by Sarah Pikul.

44

European coffee biggin, 10 1/2" tall, blue and white mottled. *Courtesy of David T. Pikul, The Chuctanunda Antique Co.* $350-400.

American coffee boiler, blue and white swirl. *Courtesy of David T. Pikul, The Chuctanunda Antique Co.* $300-350.

American funnel, "Columbian Ware," cobalt blue and white swirl. *Courtesy of Rick Jones.* $300-400. Photo by James Armstrong.

European irrigator, 9" tall, green and white swirl. *Courtesy of David T. Pikul, The Chuctanunda Antique Co.* $225-250.

European milk pail, 9" tall, blue and white marbled with a red rim. *Courtesy of David T. Pikul, The Chuctanunda Antique Co.* $150-200.

American chamber pail with lid, iris swirl. *Courtesy of Rick Jones.* $400-500. Photo by James Armstrong.

European milk boiler, 6" tall, red and white marbled with a red rim.
Courtesy of David T. Pikul, The Chuctanunda Antique Co. $250-300.

American baking pan, "Chrysolite" dark green and white swirl.
Courtesy of Rick Jones. $300-400. Photo by James Armstrong.

47

American cream can with wooden handle, cobalt blue and white swirl. *Courtesy of Rick Jones.* $700-800. Photo by James Armstrong.

American double boiler, iris swirl. *Courtesy of Rick Jones.* $300-400. Photo by James Armstrong.

European chamber pail with lid, 10" tall, green and white swirl. *Courtesy of David T. Pikul, The Chuctanunda Antique Co.* $325-400.

American coffee pot, "Columbian Ware," cobalt blue and white swirl. *Courtesy of Rick Jones.* $375-450. Photo by James Armstrong.

French lavabo, red and white mottled with a rare basin shape. *Courtesy of David T. Pikul, The Chuctanunda Antique Co.* $700-800. Photo by Sarah Pikul.

European coffee biggin, 10" tall, red and white marbled with red rims. *Courtesy of David T. Pikul, The Chuctanunda Antique Co.* $250-300.

American wall-hung soap dish, blue and white swirl. *Courtesy of David T. Pikul, The Chuctanunda Antique Co.* $150-175.

European coffee biggin, 10 1/2" tall, red and white marbled. *Courtesy of David T. Pikul, The Chuctanunda Antique Co.* $400-500.

European body pitcher, 15" tall, pink and white swirl. *Courtesy of David T. Pikul, The Chuctanunda Antique Co.* $275-325.

American bowl, "Chrysolite," dark green and white swirl. *Courtesy of Rick Jones.* $300- 375. Photo by James Armstrong.

American milk bowl, "Chrysolite," dark green and white swirl.
Courtesy of Rick Jones. $300-350. Photo by James Armstrong.

European water pitcher, 10 1/2" tall, pink and white swirl. *Courtesy of David T. Pikul, The Chuctanunda Antique Co.* $300-400.

American coffee boiler, "Chrysolite," dark green and white swirl. *Courtesy of Rick Jones.* $600-700. Photo by James Armstrong.

European chamber pail with lid and wooden handle, 10" tall, pink and white swirl. *Courtesy of David T. Pikul, The Chuctanunda Antique Co.* $300-350.

American coffee pot, cobalt blue and white swirl. *Courtesy of Rick Jones.* $300-400. Photo by James Armstrong.

European child's play set of toilette articles, blue mottled. *Courtesy of David T. Pikul, The Chuctanunda Antique Co.* $600-700. Photo by Sarah Pikul.

American kettle with lid, 8" tall, green and white swirl. *Courtesy of David T. Pikul, The Chuctanunda Antique Co.* $400-500.

European measuring pitcher, 9 1/2" tall, blue and white swirl. *Courtesy of David T. Pikul, The Chuctanunda Antique Co.* $250-300.

American berry bucket with lid and handle, gray mottled. *Courtesy of Rick Jones.* $200- 250. Photo by James Armstrong.

American chamber pail, dark green and white swirl. *Courtesy of David T. Pikul, The Chuctanunda Antique Co.* $300-350.

American salesman samples, cobalt blue and white swirl. *Courtesy of Rick Jones.* $125- 200 each. Photo by James Armstrong.

European coffee biggin, 10" tall, rare blue and pink marbled. *Courtesy of David T. Pikul, The Chuctanunda Antique Co.* $400-500.

Large European coffee biggin, 15" tall, blue and white swirl. *Courtesy of David T. Pikul, The Chuctanunda Antique Co.* $400-500.

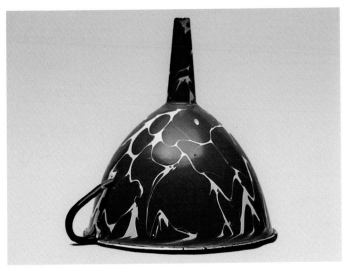

American funnel, "Columbian Ware," blue and white swirl. *Courtesy of David T. Pikul,* $300-400. Photo by James Armstrong.

European pan with lid, 4" tall, light blue and white swirl. *Courtesy of Rick Jones. The Chuctanunda Antique Co.* $175-225.

European coffee biggin, 10" tall red and white "Snow on the Mountain." *Courtesy of David T. Pikul, The Chuctanunda Antique Co.* $350-400.

French wall-hung match box, 7" tall, green and white mottled with blue lettering. *Courtesy of David T. Pikul, The Chuctanunda Antique Co.* $275-300. Photo by Sarah Pikul.

American measuring pitcher, gray mottled. *Courtesy of Rick Jones.* $200-250. Photo by James Armstrong.

German wall-hung bun keeper, blue and white chicken wire pattern. *Courtesy of David T. Pikul, The Chuctanunda Antique Co.* $225-275.

French match box, 7" tall, blue and white marbled with blue trim/ lettering. *Courtesy of David T. Pikul, The Chuctanunda Antique Co.* $200-250.

American sugar bowl with lid, gray mottled. *Courtesy of Rick Jones.* $200-250. Photo by James Armstrong.

French three-cup laundry set for soap, sand, etc., 15" long, large blue and white mottled pattern. *Courtesy of David T. Pikul, The Chuctanunda Antique Co.* $275-350.

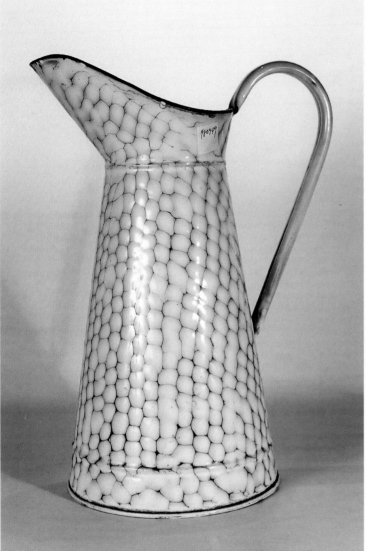

European coffee biggin, 10 1/2" tall, red and white mottled with a red handle. *Courtesy of David T. Pikul, The Chuctanunda Antique Co.* $400-500.

European body pitcher, 15" tall, blue and white chicken wire pattern. *Courtesy of David T. Pikul, The Chuctanunda Antique Co.* $350-400.

German brush bin, blue and white chicken wire pattern with blue trim/lettering. *Courtesy of David T. Pikul, The Chuctanunda Antique Co.* $250-325.

European measuring pitcher, 10 1/2" tall, blue-gray and white mottled. *Courtesy of David T. Pikul, The Chuctanunda Antique Co.* $175-225.

European body pitcher, 15" tall, blue and white "Snow on the Mountain." *Courtesy of David T. Pikul, The Chuctanunda Antique Co.* $275-350.

American ladyfinger pan, gray mottled. *Courtesy of Rick Jones.* $400-500. Photo by James Armstrong.

European chamber pail with lid and wooden handle, 10" tall, red and white mottled with red trim. *Courtesy of David T. Pikul, The Chuctanunda Antique Co.* $275-325.

French coffee biggin, 10" tall, white and brown mottled pattern with brown rims. *Courtesy of David T. Pikul, The Chuctanunda Antique Co.* $325-400. Photo by Sarah Pikul.

French wall-hung salt box with wooden lid, 10 1/2" tall, blue and white mottled with blue lettering. *Courtesy of David T. Pikul, The Chuctanunda Antique Co.* $175-225.

German wall-hung potholder bin, blue and white chicken wire pattern. *Courtesy of David T. Pikul, The Chuctanunda Antique Co.* $250-325.

European body pitcher, 15" tall, red and white mottled. *Courtesy of David T. Pikul, The Chuctanunda Antique Co.* $350-425.

European coffee biggin, 10" tall, red and white mottled with red rims. *Courtesy of David T. Pikul, The Chuctanunda Antique Co.* $400-500.

American coffee pot, 9" tall with label, gray mottled. *Courtesy of David T. Pikul, The Chuctanunda Antique Co.* $150-200.

European coffee biggin, 10" tall, light blue and white mottled. *Courtesy of David T. Pikul, The Chuctanunda Antique Co.* $175-200.

French chamber pot, 10" diameter, orange and white feathered with orange trim and a black rim. *Courtesy of David T. Pikul, The Chuctanunda Antique Co.* $175-250.

American kettle with lid and wooden handle, 9" tall, blue and white mottled. *Courtesy of David T. Pikul, The Chuctanunda Antique Co.* $225-275.

European lavabo, "End of the Day" white, blue, and green mottled. *Courtesy of David T. Pikul, The Chuctanunda Antique Co.* $700-800.

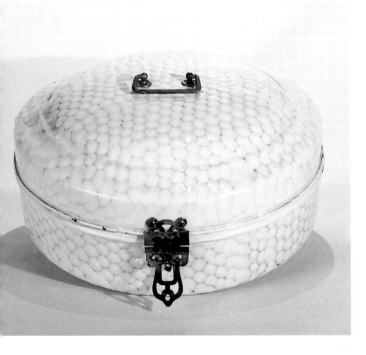

European bread box, 14" diameter, blue and white chicken wire pattern. *Courtesy of David T. Pikul, The Chuctanunda Antique Co.* $300-375.

European lunch boxes, plain white example in the center flanked by two mottled patterns. *Courtesy of David T. Pikul, The Chuctanunda Antique Co.* $65-80 each.

American kettle with steamer base, blue and white mottled. *Courtesy of David T. Pikul, The Chuctanunda Antique Co.* $200-250.

European body pitcher, 15" tall, rare sage green and white mottled. *Courtesy of David T. Pikul, The Chuctanunda Antique Co.* $300-400.

European irrigators, 9" tall, "End of the Day" coloring. *Courtesy of David T. Pikul, The Chuctanunda Antique Co.* $250-300 each.

European tea kettle, blue and white feathered with blue trim. *Courtesy of David T. Pikul, The Chuctanunda Antique Co.* $275-325.

European syrup pitcher, 6" tall, red and black in a rare, unusual pattern. *Courtesy of David T. Pikul, The Chuctanunda Antique Co.* $275-350.

American coffee pot with metal lid, 10" tall, pale blue and white mottled. *Courtesy of David T. Pikul, The Chuctanunda Antique Co.* $300-350.

European coffee biggin, 10 1/2" tall, original sticker, red, white, and blue with a chicken wire pattern. *Courtesy of David T. Pikul, The Chuctanunda Antique Co.* $400-475.

European coffee biggin, 10" tall, rare orange and blue coloring in a rare and unusual pattern. *Courtesy of David T. Pikul, The Chuctanunda Antique Co.* $600-700.

European lavabo and matching soap dish, red and white mottled. *Courtesy of David T. Pikul, The Chuctanunda Antique Co.* $800-850 for the set.

European coffee biggin, 10" tall, green and white relish pattern with an unusual textured finish. *Courtesy of David T. Pikul, The Chuctanunda Antique Co.* $275-325. Photo by Sarah Pikul.

Chapter Three
Checks, Stripes, & Other Geometrics

Specific stylistic designs have always had a strong impact on architecture and interior decor but they have influenced everyday objects as well. The perfect example is the Art Deco influence prominently displayed on the enameled ware manufactured (especially in Europe) between the late 1920s and 1940.

In sharp contrast to - and as a reaction against - the ornate fussiness associated with the interior design of the Victorian age, Art Deco was an almost immediate success. After its debut at the 1925 Paris Exhibition for Decorative Arts, curlicues and nature-inspired forms and designs were traded for geometric patterns and straight or angular, rather than curvaceous lines. Everything from enameled canister sets and milk pails to tea pots and kettles were adorned with colorful checkered patterns, stripes, and mini-print designs that almost resemble a grid pattern. It is interesting to note, however, that a great deal of the enameled ware produced with checkered graphics by German and French manufactures actually pre-dates the Art Deco Movement. In both of these countries enameled objects with cheery check designs were being turned out as early as the 1910 - 1920 period.

Stencils and tissue-paper transfers were commonly used to achieve geometric designs. Tissue-paper transfers involved the use of greasy colors and a mechanical press which applied the tissue paper to the object - paint side down - and then a roller was used to transfer the colored pattern or design to the item. Powdered enamel was then applied before additional firing took place. Stencils, on the other hand, involved the use of geometric designs cut into metal plates or heavy paper to produce designs.

The color combinations commonly found on enameled ware with Art Deco designs tend to be bright and cheerful, or bold. Examples include red and white, black and white, blue and white, yellow and white, or orange and white. Austrian firms were partial to producing matching sets for the kitchen with white stripes while other European countries favored a colored stripe on a white background. Examples of three-color combinations include red, white, yellow or white, blue, orange. Checkered patterns can be an all-over design or a small, subtle band of checks around the top of a coffee biggin. European manufacturers produced large numbers of enameled ware with Art Deco graphic designs while American firms continued to concentrate on marbled, mottled, or plainer items. This period also saw many factories continue to turn out items with floral designs and animal motifs as they proved popular for many years.

Enameled kitchen items made with a checkered design were also used as advertising premiums in France during the 1920s and 1930s. A vigorous advertising campaign by Per Lustucru noodles resulted in enameled ware with either blue and white or red and white check designs being produced for devoted housewives who clipped portions of the product packing to accumulate points. The points could then be redeemed for a checkered canister set, coffee biggin, pots and pans, and so on. The checkered objects offered by the company during the earlier years of the advertising campaign were intentionally devoid of a product mark and there's some speculation this may have been due to the tax laws. However, those items produced later, during the 1930s, sported a Lustucru logo. And logo or not, the cheerful and checkered French enameled ware of this period was long associated with the image of the portly little man and the checkered border that appeared on the Lustucru packaging. Of course enameled ware is our main concern, but it should also be noted that other checkered items used as premiums by this company included china cereal sets, painted tin canisters, etc.

Today collectors are often surprised by the wide array of geometric graphic designs featured on enameled ware but as European-made objects have found an increasingly strong niche in the world-wide collecting market, checkered patterns seem to be a popular favorite. Scarce or elaborate designs will naturally have increased value over more common examples but generally any enameled object with a detailed graphic design will fetch a premium price.

Austrian toilette set including a large water pitcher and basin, soap dish, and two covered dishes for combs and toothbrushes. Set is white with black stripes (stenciled) and a hand-painted design. *Courtesy of David T. Pikul, The Chuctanunda Antique Co.* $1000-1200.

European coffee biggin, 10" tall, orange with black trim and a black/white check design. *Courtesy of David T. Pikul, The Chuctanunda Antique Co.* $350-400. Photo by Sarah Pikul.

European milk pail, 10" tall, olive green with a white/green check design. *Courtesy of David T. Pikul, The Chuctanunda Antique Co.* $175-225.

French six-piece canister set, graduating sizes, French lettering, white with red trim and a red/white check pattern. *Courtesy of David T. Pikul, The Chuctanunda Antique Co.* $500-600.

European coffee biggin, 10 1/2" tall, white with a striped design. *Courtesy of David T. Pikul, The Chuctanunda Antique Co.* $300-400.

European wall-hung match box, 7" tall, red and white stripes combined with a petite floral design. *Courtesy of David T. Pikul, The Chuctanunda Antique Co.* $250-275.

European wall-hung utensil rack, 14" wide by 19" long, "French blue" with a red check design. *Courtesy of David T. Pikul, The Chuctanunda Antique Co.* $400-500.

Large European coffee biggin, 14" tall, double handles, "French blue" with bands of geometric designs. *Courtesy of David T. Pikul, The Chuctanunda Antique Co.* $650-750.

European teapot and matching sugar bowl, red and white grid pattern. *Courtesy of David T. Pikul, The Chuctanunda Antique Co.* $200-250 each.

European measuring pitcher, 9" tall, white with green shaded stripes/lines. *Courtesy of David T. Pikul, The Chuctanunda Antique Co.* $275-300.

European coffee biggin, 10 1/2" tall, orange and white droopy check pattern with red trim. *Courtesy of David T. Pikul, The Chuctanunda Antique Co.* $400-500.

French five-piece canister set, graduating sizes, orange with black trim and geometric design. *Courtesy of David T. Pikul, The Chuctanunda Antique Co.* $400-500.

French six-piece canister set, rare shape, light blue with striping. *Courtesy of Pam DeBisschop.* $500-600.

European coffee pot, 9 1/2" tall, white with brown shading and graphic design. *Courtesy of David T. Pikul, The Chuctanunda Antique Co.* $150-200.

European mustard pot with lid and saucer, white with a blue graphic design. *Courtesy of David T. Pikul, The Chuctanunda Antique Co.* $175-200.

French coffee biggin, 10 1/2" tall, red with white band and graphic design. *Courtesy of David T. Pikul, The Chuctanunda Antique Co.* $275-350.

European wall-hung lavabo, tank 10" wide and basin has a 13" diameter, red and white Art Deco Design. *Courtesy of David T. Pikul, The Chuctanunda Antique Co.* $600-700.

European four-piece canister set, red and white stripes with a floral band, French lettering. *Courtesy of David T. Pikul, The Chuctanunda Antique Co.* $350-400.

European coffee biggin, 10 1/2" tall, white with red graphic design. *Courtesy of David T. Pikul, The Chuctanunda Antique Co.* $350-400.

French milk pail, 10" tall, red with white check design. *Courtesy of David T. Pikul, The Chuctanunda Antique Co.* $250-300.

European coffee biggin, 10" tall, white with brown shading, blue rim, and blue/white graphic design. *Courtesy of David T. Pikul, The Chuctanunda Antique Co.* $275-350.

European wall-hung utensil rack with tool, 12" wide by 19" long, Art Deco design. *Courtesy of David T. Pikul, The Chuctanunda Antique Co.* $300-400.

European coffee pot, 9" tall, white with light blue shading and blue graphic design. *Courtesy of David T. Pikul, The Chuctanunda Antique Co.* $150-200.

French wall-hung salt box, 10" tall, white with red checkered band and red lettering. *Courtesy of David T. Pikul, The Chuctanunda Antique Co.* $275-325.

French five-piece canister set, graduating sizes, white with brown and orange graphic design. *Courtesy of David T. Pikul, The Chuctanunda Antique Co.* $400-450.

European coffee biggin, 12" tall, modernistic styling (note handle and spout), brown and white Art Deco design. *Courtesy of David T. Pikul, The Chuctanunda Antique Co.* $350-400.

European coffee biggin, 10" tall, orange with black graphic design. *Courtesy of David T. Pikul, The Chuctanunda Antique Co.* $275-350.

French wall-hung salt box, 10" tall, white with red/white grid pattern and red lettering. *Courtesy of David T. Pikul, The Chuctanunda Antique Co.* $250-300.

Large French coffee biggin, 14" tall, double handles, white with red trim and red/white check design. *Courtesy of David T. Pikul, The Chuctanunda Antique Co.* $400-500.

Two French match boxes, both 7" tall, red and white with a check design. *Courtesy of David T. Pikul, The Chuctanunda Antique Co.* $250-300 each.

French six-piece canister set, graduating sizes, white and red shading with white graphic design. *Courtesy of Pam DeBisschop.* $500-600.

French six-piece canister set, graduating sizes, rare color combination of green with yellow checks and lettering. *Courtesy of David T. Pikul, The Chuctanunda Antique Co.* $700- 800.

French water pitcher and matching basin, white with black trim and check design. *Courtesy of David T. Pikul, The Chuctanunda Antique Co.* $350-425.

French water pitcher, white with red and white check band. *Courtesy of David T. Pikul, The Chuctanunda Antique Co.* $250-325.

European coffee biggin, 9 1/2" tall, red and white stripes with a floral band. *Courtesy of David T. Pikul, The Chuctanunda Antique Co.* $350-425.

European coffee biggin, 10 1/2" tall, white and yellow graphic design. *Courtesy of David T. Pikul, The Chuctanunda Antique Co.* $350-400.

French coffee biggin, 10 1/2" tall, white with blue and white checkered design. *Courtesy of David T. Pikul, The Chuctanunda Antique Co.* $350-400.

French salt box, 10" tall, red with red/white band of checks and white lettering. *Courtesy of David T. Pikul, The Chuctanunda Antique Co.* $250-300.

European coffee biggin, 10" tall, marked "B&B," yellow with yellow/white stripes. *Courtesy of David T. Pikul, The Chuctanunda Antique Co.* $350-400.

Three European footed trivets, 9" size, red, blue, and yellow check patterns. *Courtesy of David T. Pikul, The Chuctanunda Antique Co.* $75-100 each.

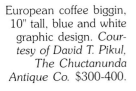

European coffee biggin, 10" tall, blue and white graphic design. *Courtesy of David T. Pikul, The Chuctanunda Antique Co.* $300-400.

European milk pail, 10" tall, red with black/white graphic design. *Courtesy of David T. Pikul, The Chuctanunda Antique Co.* $225-275.

European pot with lid and handles, 6" tall, white with red striping. *Courtesy of David T. Pikul, The Chuctanunda Antique Co.* $175-250.

French six-piece canister set, white with red shading creating a striped design. *Courtesy of Pam DeBisschop.* $400-500.

French wall-hung utensil rack with single tool, red with a red/white check design. *Courtesy of David T. Pikul, The Chuctanunda Antique Co.* $350-400.

Another French utensil rack with red and white checks. Compare to previous photo and note the difference in appearance depending upon the predominant color. *Courtesy of David T. Pikul, The Chuctanunda Antique Co.* $350-400.

French wall-hung salt box, 10" tall, white with blue shading creating a graphic design. *Courtesy of David T. Pikul, The Chuctanunda Antique Co.* $200-300.

European body pitcher, 15" tall, red/blue graphic design. *Courtesy of David T. Pikul, The Chuctanunda Antique Co.* $275-350.

European coffee biggin, 10" tall, tan with brown shading and graphic design. *Courtesy of David T. Pikul, The Chuctanunda Antique Co.* $200-275.

European coffee biggin, 10 1/2" tall, white with angular blue stripes and red rims. *Courtesy of David T. Pikul, The Chuctanunda Antique Co.* $300-400.

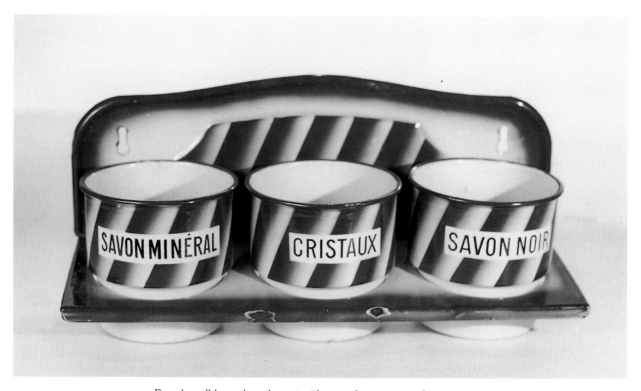

French wall-hung laundry set with cups for soap, sand, etc.,
15" wide, white with brown shading/stripes. *Courtesy of David T.
Pikul, The Chuctanunda Antique Co.* $200-300.

French salt box, 10" tall, red with a wooden lid, red/
white striping, and white lettering. *Courtesy of David
T. Pikul, The Chuctanunda Antique Co.* $200-300.

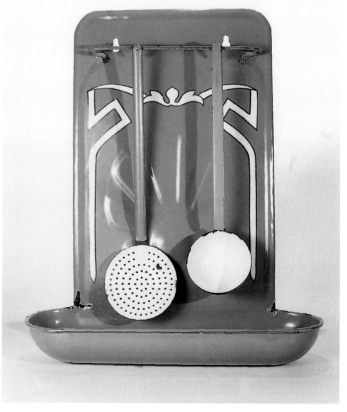

European wall-hung utensil rack with two tools, 14" wide by
19" long, "French blue" with white graphic design. *Courtesy of
David T. Pikul, The Chuctanunda Antique Co.* $300-400.

European coffee pot, 9" tall, with red/white/black graphic design. *Courtesy of David T. Pikul, The Chuctanunda Antique Co.* $175-250.

European coffee pot, 9" tall, light green with dark green/yellow graphic design. *Courtesy of David T. Pikul, The Chuctanunda Antique Co.* $150-200.

French five-piece canister set, graduating sizes, red with black/white check design. *Courtesy of David T. Pikul, The Chuctanunda Antique Co.* $500-600.

European body pitcher, 15" tall, blue and white shading with geometric design. *Courtesy of David T. Pikul, The Chuctanunda Antique Co.* $200-300.

French wall-hung salt box, 10" tall, white with a red/blue shaded striped design. *Courtesy of David T. Pikul, The Chuctanunda Antique Co.* $275-325. Photo by Sarah Pikul.

European coffee biggin, 10 1/2" tall, cream color with an orange/black graphic design. *Courtesy of David T. Pikul, The Chuctanunda Antique Co.* $400-500.

European coffee biggin, 9 1/2" tall, white with a green/yellow graphic design. *Courtesy of David T. Pikul, The Chuctanunda Antique Co.* $275-325.

European coffee biggin, 10 1/2" tall, marked "B&B," white with blue/white graphic design. *Courtesy of David T. Pikul, The Chuctanunda Antique Co.* $350-400.

French clock, white with blue striping and numbers. *Courtesy of David T. Pikul, The Chuctanunda Antique Co.* $275-350.

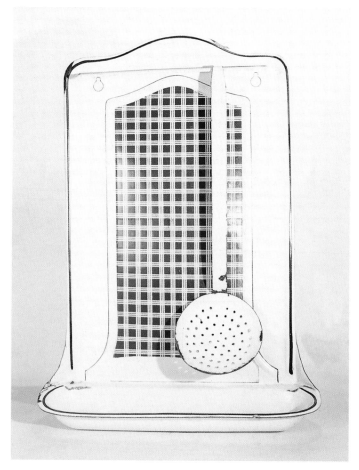

European coffee biggin, 10 1/2" tall, red/yellow graphic design with white spout and handle. *Courtesy of David T. Pikul, The Chuctanunda Antique Co.* $250-300.

European wall-hung utensil rack with single tool, 12" wide by 19" long, white with blue/white check design. *Courtesy of David T. Pikul, The Chuctanunda Antique Co.* $225-275.

European footed colander and matching salt box with wooden lid, red with black/white graphic design and white lettering. *Courtesy of David T. Pikul, The Chuctanunda Antique Co.* $250-300 each.

European chocolate pot. Rare 5" size, wooden handle, white and blue striping. *Courtesy of David T. Pikul, The Chuctanunda Antique Co.* $275-350.

European teapot, 4" tall, light blue with a blue/white graphic design. *Courtesy of David T. Pikul, The Chuctanunda Antique Co.* $150-175.

French coffee biggin, 10" tall, "French blue" with red trim and a white band of checks. *Courtesy of David T. Pikul, The Chuctanunda Antique Co.* $350-400.

European coffee biggin, 11" tall, red/white/green shading/graphic design. *Courtesy of David T. Pikul, The Chuctanunda Antique Co.* $350-400.

Large European coffee biggin, 14" tall, double handles, striped design. *Courtesy of David T. Pikul, The Chuctanunda Antique Co.* $300-400.

European syrup pitcher, 5" tall, marked "B&B," red/white graphic design. *Courtesy of David T. Pikul, The Chuctanunda Antique Co.* $250-300.

French salt box, 10" tall, wooden lid, white with a check design. *Courtesy of David T. Pikul, The Chuctanunda Antique Co.* $250-300.

European syrup pitcher, 4" tall, unusual shape, white with red trim and a check design. *Courtesy of David T. Pikul, The Chuctanunda Antique Co.* $275-325.

French six-piece canister set, graduating sizes, red with white lettering and a black/white graphic design. *Courtesy of David T. Pikul, The Chuctanunda Antique Co.* $500-600. Photo by Sarah Pikul.

Matching European pans, graduating sizes, red with white checks. *Courtesy of David T. Pikul, The Chuctanunda Antique Co.* $300-350 for the set.

European teapot, 6" tall, white with green trim and circular design. *Courtesy of David T. Pikul, The Chuctanunda Antique Co.* $150-175.

European coffee biggin, 10 1/2" tall, white with red trim and a check design. *Courtesy of David T. Pikul, The Chuctanunda Antique Co.* $300-400.

European teapot, 5" tall, black with yellow graphic design. *Courtesy of David T. Pikul, The Chuctanunda Antique Co.* $175-225.

European coffee biggin, 10 1/2" tall, white with red trim and a red check design. *Courtesy of David T. Pikul, The Chuctanunda Antique Co.* $350-425.

European pot with lid, 10" diameter, white with blue check design. *Courtesy of David T. Pikul, The Chuctanunda Antique Co.* $250-300.

French five-piece canister set, graduating sizes, white with a red graphic design. *Courtesy of David T. Pikul, The Chuctanunda Antique Co.* $400-500.

European coffee pot, 9" tall, light brown with black trim and stripes. *Courtesy of David T. Pikul, The Chuctanunda Antique Co.* $150-200.

European coffee biggin, 10 1/2" tall, rare red and white droopy check pattern. *Courtesy of David T. Pikul, The Chuctanunda Antique Co.* $500-600.

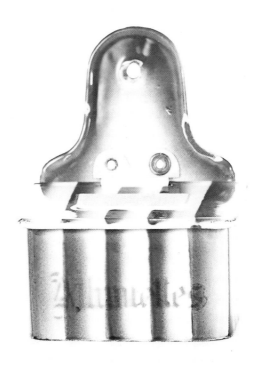

European wall-hung match box, 7" tall, white with blue stripes and French lettering in red. *Courtesy of David T. Pikul, The Chuctanunda Antique Co.* $175-250.

European coffee biggin, 10 1/2" tall, brown and white stripes. *Courtesy of David T. Pikul, The Chuctanunda Antique Co.* $250-300.

European wall-hung salt box, 10" tall, white with a red/white check pattern and French lettering in red. *Courtesy of David T. Pikul, The Chuctanunda Antique Co.* $225-300.

French colander, white with a red check design. *Courtesy of David T. Pikul, The Chuctanunda Antique Co.* $175-225.

French six-piece canister set, white with blue/red shading/stripe design. *Courtesy of David T. Pikul, The Chuctanunda Antique Co.* $500-600.

European wall-hung match box, 7" tall, light blue with a cobalt/white graphic design and French lettering. *Courtesy of David T. Pikul, The Chuctanunda Antique Co.* $150-200.

French coffee pot, 10" tall, medium blue with a red/white graphic design. *Courtesy of David T. Pikul, The Chuctanunda Antique Co.* $300-400.

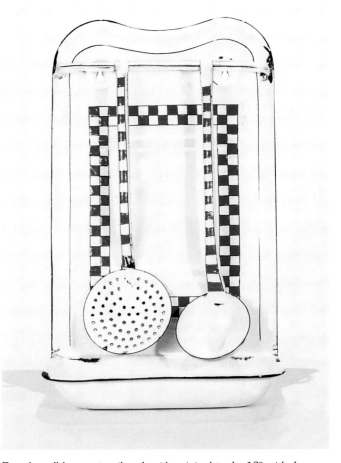

French wall-hung utensil rack with original tools, 12" wide by 19" long, white with a red check design. *Courtesy of David T. Pikul, The Chuctanunda Antique Co.* $350-500.

French kettle with lid, 10" size, large red and white check design - possibly a *Lustucru* advertising premium. *Courtesy of David T. Pikul, The Chuctanunda Antique Co.* $300-350.

Large European coffee biggin, 14" tall, light and dark brown stripes. *Courtesy of David T. Pikul, The Chuctanunda Antique Co.* $300-400.

European wall-hung utensil rack, 12" wide by 19" long, yellow and white droopy check pattern. *Courtesy of David T. Pikul, The Chuctanunda Antique Co.* $300-350.

French five-piece canister set, graduating sizes, blue with black/white graphic design and white lettering. *Courtesy of David T. Pikul, The Chuctanunda Antique Co.* $500-600.

French wall-hung utensil rack with two tools, red with a red/white check border. *Courtesy of David T. Pikul, The Chuctanunda Antique Co.* $225-275.

European milk pail, 10" tall, medium blue with a white check design. *Courtesy of David T. Pikul, The Chuctanunda Antique Co.* $150-200.

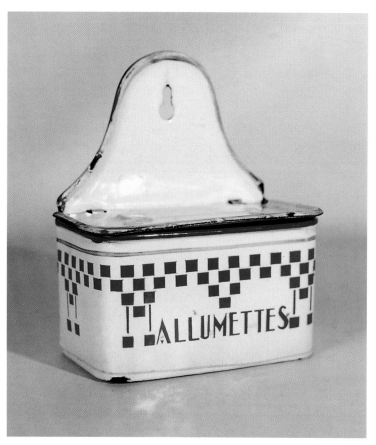

French wall-hung match box, 7" tall, white with red checks and lettering. *Courtesy of David T. Pikul, The Chuctanunda Antique Co.* $200-275.

European coffee biggin, 10 1/2" tall, red with band of white checks. *Courtesy of David T. Pikul, The Chuctanunda Antique Co.* $300-350.

European trivets, one with a rare green and white diamond pattern and the other blue and white with stripes and a floral design. *Courtesy of David T. Pikul, The Chuctanunda Antique Co.* Green/white trivet $150-200 and blue and white trivet $125-150.

French three-piece coffee set, 7 1/2" tall, white with a blue check design. *Courtesy of David T. Pikul, The Chuctanunda Antique Co.* $350-400.

European syrup pitcher, 5" tall, marked "B&B" with a red/white graphic design. *Courtesy of David T. Pikul, The Chuctanunda Antique Co.* $275-300.

French wall-hung match box, 7" tall, orange with a check design and white lettering. *Courtesy of David T. Pikul, The Chuctanunda Antique Co.* $200-275.

European water pitcher and matching basin, yellow with a yellow/ black check pattern. *Courtesy of Pam DeBisschop.* $300-400.

European coffee pot, 12" tall, blue and white shading/graphic design. *Courtesy of David T. Pikul, The Chuctanunda Antique Co.* $200-275.

German wall-hung laundry set with cups for soap, sand, etc., 16" wide, white with a blue graphic design and brown lettering. *Courtesy of David T. Pikul, The Chuctanunda Antique Co.* $400-450.

of matching pans, red with white checks. *Courtesy Chuctanunda Antique Co.* $225-300 for the set.

French measuring pitcher, 9" tall, brown and white check pattern. *Courtesy of David T. Pikul, The Chuctanunda Antique Co.* $150-200.

French wall-hung utensil rack with single tool, 12" wide by 19" long, white with red trim and check design. *Courtesy of David T. Pikul, The Chuctanunda Antique Co.* $275-325.

European wall-hung laundry set, marked "B&B," 15" wide, white with a red graphic design. *Courtesy of David T. Pikul, The Chuctanunda Antique Co.* $275-350.

French wall-hung salt box with wooden lid, 10" tall, white with a red check design. *Courtesy of David T. Pikul, The Chuctanunda Antique Co.* $200-250.

European milk pail, 10" tall, orange with a black/white check design. *Courtesy of David T. Pikul, The Chuctanunda Antique Co.* $200-275.

French wall-hung salt box, 10" tall, white with a blue/yellow check design. *Courtesy of David T. Pikul, The Chuctanunda Antique Co.* $300-400.

European coffee biggin, 12" tall, white with blue shading/check design. *Courtesy of David T. Pikul, The Chuctanunda Antique Co.* $375-450.

European coffee pot, 9" tall, brown with a geometric design. *Courtesy of David T. Pikul, The Chuctanunda Antique Co.* $200-250.

European wall-hung match box, 7" tall, marked "B&B," white with a blue/white graphic design. *Courtesy of David T. Pikul, The Chuctanunda Antique Co.* $150-200.

European coffee biggin, 12" tall, white with light blue shading/checkered pattern. *Courtesy of David T. Pikul, The Chuctanunda Antique Co.* $350-425.

French five-piece canister set, graduating sizes, red with a red/white graphic design. *Courtesy of David T. Pikul, The Chuctanunda Antique Co.* $400-500.

European syrup pitcher, 5" tall, red and white droopy check. *Courtesy of Pam DeBisschop.* $300-350.

European coffee pot, 10 1/2" tall, white with red trim and a large red/white check pattern -possibly a *Lustucru* advertising premium. *Courtesy of David T. Pikul, The Chuctanunda Antique Co.* $300-400.

European milk pails, 10" tall, one red and white striped, the other blue and white striped. *Courtesy of David T. Pikul, The Chuctanunda Antique Co.* $200-250 each.

European wall-hung match box, 7" tall, marked "B&B," white with a yellow lid and yellow/white stripes. *Courtesy of David T. Pikul, The Chuctanunda Antique Co.* $225-250.

French five-piece canister set, graduating sizes, large red and white check pattern - possibly a *Lustucru* advertising premium. *Courtesy of David T. Pikul, The Chuctanunda Antique Co.* $600-700. Photo by Sarah Pikul.

European coffee pot, 9" tall, black with wavy yellow stripes. *Courtesy of David T. Pikul, The Chuctanunda Antique Co.* $350-400.

French wall-hung match box, 7" tall, white with a red/white check band. *Courtesy of David T. Pikul, The Chuctanunda Antique Co.* $225-250.

European coffee biggin, 10" tall, white with blue shading/stripes. *Courtesy of David T. Pikul, The Chuctanunda Antique Co.* $300-350.

European coffee biggin, 10" tall, modernistic shape, blue and white shading with an Art Deco design. *Courtesy of David T. Pikul, The Chuctanunda Antique Co.* $350-400.

European coffee biggin, 10 1/2" tall, marked "B&B," white with a red graphic design. *Courtesy of David T. Pikul, The Chuctanunda Antique Co.* $350-400.

European measuring pitcher and matching coffee pot, cream with
a checkered graphic design. *Courtesy of David T. Pikul, The
Chuctanunda Antique Co.* $175-200 each.

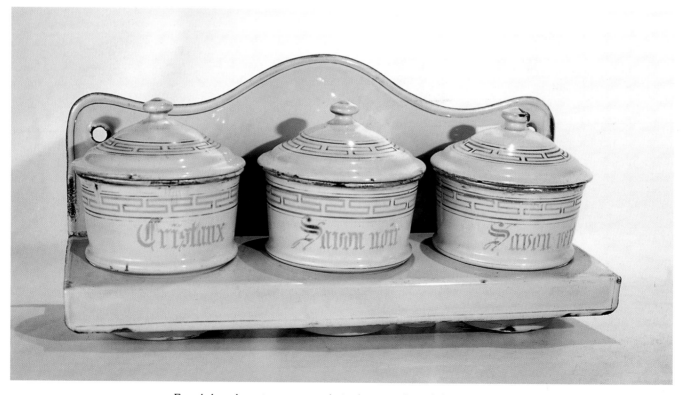

French laundry set, rare example in that cups have lids, cream
with gilt trim, geometric motif, and French lettering. *Courtesy of
David T. Pikul, The Chuctanunda Antique Co.* $250- 300.

French kettle with lid, "French blue" with a red rim and white checks. *Courtesy of David T. Pikul, The Chuctanunda Antique Co.* $225-300. Photo by Sarah Pikul.

French footed bowl, 5" diameter, green and white shading with a dark green graphic design. *Courtesy of David T. Pikul, The Chuctanunda Antique Co.* $75-100.

French wall-hung utensil rack with an unusual scalloped drip basin, white with a blue checkered design. *Courtesy of David T. Pikul, The Chuctanunda Antique Co.* $375-400.

Chapter Four
Flowers, Birds, Etc.

In an attempt to beautify enameled ware, just as ceramics were embellished with floral and nature motifs, European manufacturers began decorating their utilitarian housewares during the second half of the nineteenth century. Specific stylistic designs are evident from examining older pieces of decorative enameled ware. For example, during the 1860s and 1870s many luxury items as well as objects intended for home use were colored blue, black, or ivory and adorned with ribbons, gilt trim, and floral bouquets - a style commonly referred to as Boudoir. During the 1870s - 1890s many firms continued to employ artists to hand-paint designs (using ceramic or enamel paints) composed mainly of floral motifs (roses or wildflowers) and birds or butterflies. In old European countries religious cards and decorative prints often proved the inspiration for many of the hand-painted flowers during this time period but the Oriental influence popular in home decor during the 1890s also brought colorful birds and a touch of the exotic to enameled ware. Landscapes and the windmill scenes so often associated with Dutch and Scandinavian countries were also a popular means of decorating enameled goods during the last quarter of the nineteenth century. Done in blue and white, these designs often imitated the Delft tiles long used in northern European homes and symbolic of cleanliness. And certainly not to be forgotten, the stylized flowers and curves that predominated decoration during the turn-of-the-century Art Nouveau period.

Eventually cost-effective measures, new technology, and demands for increased production resulted in decorative designs being achieved via chromolithography, stamps, silk screening, tissue-paper transfers, and decals. A certain level of skill was still required to achieve pleasing results, especially with the stamps that created an outline to be filled in by hand. Gilt trim (usually in the form of thin striping) also continued to be done by hand. Collectors will note that many of the objects made in France were adorned with a combination of petite garlands of roses and gilt trim.

While European manufacturers routinely produced enameled ware with beautiful decorations and designs (in imitation of costlier ceramics), floral and nature motifs used on American-made enameled ware during the late 1800s were targeted for the high end of the market - those items used in the Victorian dining room rather than the kitchen. Such items (for example, coffee or tea pots) were also trimmed in pewter or other metals and were sold to compete with the better dinnerware made of ceramics or silver-plate. Such designs were created with colorful decals and it wasn't until the late 1920s and the 1930s that decals with floral motifs were used again on assorted "lines" of enameled ware produced to appeal to housewives with cheerful and colorful kitchens.

Enameled objects with floral/nature designs and landscape scenes are striking and beautiful. Collectors are drawn to these decorative items and often try to collect matching pieces to build a set. Prices for such items range at the higher end of the market, especially for those designs considered quite popular or rare. One such example are the European pieces with blue striping and garlands of roses.

French water pitcher with a flared rim, 10" tall, white with a pink daisy floral design. *Courtesy of David T. Pikul, The Chuctanunda Antique Co.* $275-325.

French three-piece canister set for coffee, 7 1/2" tall, pink and white with a floral design and French lettering. *Courtesy of Pam DeBisschop.* $400-500.

European wall-hung salt box with a wooden lid, 10" tall, air-brushed floral design and blue lettering. *Courtesy of David T. Pikul, The Chuctanunda Antique Co.* $225-250.

European (Belgium or French) teapot, 3" tall, blue with a floral design. *Courtesy of David T. Pikul, The Chuctanunda Antique Co.* $350-400.

American coffee set, white with floral design and metal trim/lids. Set includes a large and small coffee pot, sugar bowl with lid, and creamer. *Courtesy of David T. Pikul, The Chuctanunda Antique Co.* $1800-2000 for the set.

Yugoslovian tray, white interior, yellow exterior with a floral design and black rim. *Courtesy of David T. Pikul, The Chuctanunda Antique Co.* $125-150.

French pitcher, 13" tall, white with a rose design. *Courtesy of David T. Pikul, The Chuctanunda Antique Co.* $200-300.

European coffee mug, 4" tall, white interior and pink exterior with a floral design. *Courtesy of David T. Pikul, The Chuctanunda Antique Co.* $60-80.

French teapot, 4" tall, white with pink shading and a rose design. *Courtesy of David T. Pikul, The Chuctanunda Antique Co.* $300-350.

French body pitcher, 15" tall, blue with a floral design. *Courtesy of David T. Pikul, The Chuctanunda Antique Co.* $300-400.

French utensil rack with two tools, 14" wide by 19" long, white with blue shading and a floral motif. *Courtesy of David T. Pikul, The Chuctanunda Antique Co.* $300-400.

American chamber pot, marked "Made in West Virginia," white with pale green shading, black handle, and floral design. *Courtesy of David T. Pikul, The Chuctanunda Antique Co.* $275- 350.

American butter dish, 5" tall, white with metal trim and floral design on lid. *Courtesy of David T. Pikul, The Chuctanunda Antique Co.* $350-425.

European sugar bowl, 4" tall, black with a daisy design. *Courtesy of David T. Pikul, The Chuctanunda Antique Co.* $225-275.

French chamber pail or lidded bucket with pastel shading and floral design. *Courtesy of David T. Pikul, The Chuctanunda Antique Co.* $350-400.

Three European pitchers in the "French blue" color. The large body pitcher, 15" tall, is white with blue shading and an iris floral design. A 10" measuring pitcher has a blue mottled pattern and the smaller measuring pitcher, 8" tall, is a blue and white droopy check with a red rim. *Courtesy of Ellen M. Plante.* Body pitcher $375-425, 10" pitcher $150-175, and 8" droopy check pitcher $300-350. Photo by Ted Plante.

European coffee pot, 9" tall, white with a large floral motif. *Courtesy of David T. Pikul, The Chuctanunda Antique Co.* $275-300.

European wall-hung salt box with French lettering, 10" tall, blue and white striped with a garland of roses. *Courtesy of David T. Pikul, The Chuctanunda Antique Co.* $275-325.

French coffee biggin, 12" tall, double handles, a rare shape with white, pink, and blue shading/floral motif. *Courtesy of David T. Pikul, The Chuctanunda Antique Co.* $800-900.

French coffee pot with hinged lid, 9" tall, white with a floral motif and gilt trim. *Courtesy of David T. Pikul, The Chuctanunda Antique Co.* $300-375.

French utensil rack, rare 19" by 19" size, white with a bird/floral design. *Courtesy of David T. Pikul, The Chuctanunda Antique Co.* $400-500.

European coffee biggin, 10 1/2" tall, white with a petite floral band. *Courtesy of David T. Pikul, The Chuctanunda Antique Co.* $275-350.

European measuring pitcher, 10" tall, pale blue with a bird design. *Courtesy of David T. Pikul, The Chuctanunda Antique Co.* $250-300.

American coffee pot, 10" tall, cobalt blue with a white floral design. *Courtesy of David T. Pikul, The Chuctanunda Antique Co.* $350-400.

Early French lavabo, tear-drop shape, dispenser and basin both 13" wide with a matching soap dish. Lavabo is cream with a blue floral motif and gilt trim. *Courtesy of David T. Pikul, The Chuctanunda Antique Co.* $800-1000.

A close-up of the lavabo in the previous photo to illustrate the unusual water spigot crafted to resemble a dragon head.

German water pitcher, 12" tall, marked "Germany." Pitcher has a white interior and white/yellow shading on the exterior with a large floral design. *Courtesy of Ellen M. Plante.* $375-450. Photo by Ted Plante.

European coffee pot, 10" tall, pink with a red rim and a floral design. *Courtesy of David T. Pikul, The Chuctanunda Antique Co.* $300-400.

European measuring pitcher, 11" tall, white with a blue daisy design. *Courtesy of David T. Pikul, The Chuctanunda Antique Co.* $275-325.

European coffee pot, 10" tall, white with pink shading and a floral bouquet. *Courtesy of David T. Pikul, The Chuctanunda Antique Co.* $300-400.

124

German wall-hung onion keeper, white with blue scenic design. *Courtesy of David T. Pikul, The Chuctanunda Antique Co.* $275-325.

German wall-hung flour box with a wooden lid, 11" tall, white with a blue windmill design. *Courtesy of David T. Pikul, The Chuctanunda Antique Co.* $250-300.

French coffee biggin, 10 1/2" tall, rare green with a floral design and gilt trim. *Courtesy of David T. Pikul, The Chuctanunda Antique Co.* $400-500.

European irrigator, 9" tall, white with a floral design. *Courtesy of David T. Pikul, The Chuctanunda Antique Co.* $175-225.

Large French coffee biggin, 14" tall, white with blue shading and a rose design. *Courtesy of David T. Pikul, The Chuctanunda Antique Co.* $500-600.

European milk pail with lid and handle, 10" tall, white with a blue graphic design. *Courtesy of David T. Pikul, The Chuctanunda Antique Co.* $225-275.

French pitcher with hinged lid, 9" tall, white with a floral motif and gilt trim. *Courtesy of David T. Pikul, The Chuctanunda Antique Co.* $375-425.

French pitcher, 10" tall, white with a red rim and floral design. *Courtesy of David T. Pikul, The Chuctanunda Antique Co.* $275-350.

French wall-hung utensil rack, 12" wide by 19" long, white with blue shading and a floral design. *Courtesy of David T. Pikul, The Chuctanunda Antique Co.* $300-375.

European teapot, 6" tall, black with a stylized floral design. *Courtesy of David T. Pikul, The Chuctanunda Antique Co.* $275-325.

French coffee biggin, 10 1/2" tall, white with a floral design. *Courtesy of David T. Pikul, The Chuctanunda Antique Co.* $325-375.

French six-piece canister set, white/blue shading with a floral design and French lettering. *Courtesy of Pam DeBisschop.* $700-800.

European coffee pot, 10" tall, rare cobalt blue with a raised floral design. *Courtesy of David T. Pikul, The Chuctanunda Antique Co.* $500-600.

European utensil rack, 12" wide by 19" long, white with blue trim and a floral design. *Courtesy of David T. Pikul, The Chuctanunda Antique Co.* Utensil rack $275-300 and spatula $125-150.

Above: German bowl, 3" tall, pale green with a red rim and daisy design. *Courtesy of David T. Pikul, The Chuctanunda Antique Co.* $100-125.

Left: French coffee biggin, 10 1/2" tall, "French blue" with red rims, gilt trim, and floral design. *Courtesy of David T. Pikul, The Chuctanunda Antique Co.* $400-500.

French set of pots and pans with lids, graduating sizes, dusty rose color with a floral design. *Courtesy of David T. Pikul, The Chuctanunda Antique Co.* $700-800 for the set.

French measuring pitcher, rare black with a white floral design. Note the flat handle, which is an indication of early construction. *Courtesy of David T. Pikul, The Chuctanunda Antique Co.* $300-350.

European (possibly German) coffee pot, 10" tall, white with red shading and a large floral design. *Courtesy of David T. Pikul, The Chuctanunda Antique Co.* $275-350.

French chocolate pot with a wooden handle, 10" tall, white with a floral band and gilt trim. *Courtesy of David T. Pikul, The Chuctanunda Antique Co.* $350-400.

European teapot, red and cobalt blue shading with a floral design and ornate gilt trim. *Courtesy of Pam DeBisschop.* $275-350.

French coffee biggin, 10" tall, with matching creamer. Both pieces are white with a petite blue floral design. *Courtesy of David T. Pikul, The Chuctanunda Antique Co.* Biggin $400-500 and creamer $225-250.

French coffee biggin, 10 1/2" tall, rare green with a floral design and gilt trim. *Courtesy of David T. Pikul, The Chuctanunda Antique Co.* $400-500.

Rare and unusual French watering can, 18" tall, white with a red rim and cherry design. *Courtesy of David T. Pikul, The Chuctanunda Antique Co.* $500-600.

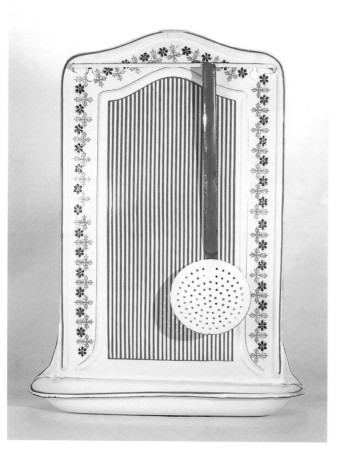

French body pitcher, 15" tall, white with a floral design. *Courtesy of David T. Pikul, The Chuctanunda Antique Co.* $300-400.

French wall-hung utensil rack with a single tool, 12" wide by 19" long, white with a stripe design and floral border. *Courtesy of David T. Pikul, The Chuctanunda Antique Co.* $300-400.

French coffee biggin, 10 1/2" tall, white with red trim and a hand-painted floral design. *Courtesy of David T. Pikul, The Chuctanunda Antique Co.* $500-600.

European coffee pot, 10" tall, white with red shading and floral design. *Courtesy of David T. Pikul, The Chuctanunda Antique Co.* $275-325.

132

French salt box with wooden lid, 10" tall, white with blue shading, French lettering, and a floral design. *Courtesy of Pam DeBisschop.* $300-400.

French coffee pot, 9 1/2" tall, "French blue" with a floral design. *Courtesy of David T. Pikul, The Chuctanunda Antique Co.* $300-400.

European child-size chamber pot, 4" tall, light green with Dutch figures and a windmill scene. *Courtesy of David T. Pikul, The Chuctanunda Antique Co.* $100-125.

French coffee pot, 10" tall, white with gilt trim and a hand-painted floral design. *Courtesy of David T. Pikul, The Chuctanunda Antique Co.* $275-300.

133

Two Czechoslovakian pitchers with hinged lids, 12" and 10" tall, cream color with a verse/landscape scene. *Courtesy of David T. Pikul, The Chuctanunda Antique Co.* $300-350 each.

European teapot, 4" tall, white with a landscape scene. *Courtesy of David T. Pikul, The Chuctanunda Antique Co.* $225-275.

European coffee pot, 9" tall, brown shading with a holly motif. *Courtesy of David T. Pikul, The Chuctanunda Antique Co.* $300-375.

Early European body pitcher, 15" tall, pale yellow with a hand-painted floral/cornucopia design. *Courtesy of Ellen M. Plante* $375-425. Photo by Ted Plante.

European coffee biggin, 10 1/2" tall, cream with light green shading and floral design. *Courtesy of David T. Pikul, The Chuctanunda Antique Co.* $175-250.

European coffee biggin, 10 1/2" tall, white with red trim and a cherry motif. *Courtesy of David T. Pikul, The Chuctanunda Antique Co.* $400-500.

European bucket, 12" tall, white with blue/orange shading and a palm tree/building scene. *Courtesy of David T. Pikul, The Chuctanunda Antique Co.* $350-400.

Matching French water pitcher and basin, white with blue shading and a wildflower design. *Courtesy of David T. Pikul, The Chuctanunda Antique Co.* $325-400.

Early French footed bowl with perforations, white and blue shading with red trim and a floral design. *Courtesy of David T. Pikul, The Chuctanunda Antique Co.* $350-400.

German canisters, white with a landscape scene and German lettering. *Courtesy of David T. Pikul, The Chuctanunda Antique Co.* $175-225 for the pair.

136

European teapot, 4" tall, multicolored with rare design. *Courtesy of David T. Pikul, The Chuctanunda Antique Co.* $350-400.

European wall-hung utensil rack with two tools, 12" wide by 19" tall, white with a landscape scene. *Courtesy of David T. Pikul, The Chuctanunda Antique Co.* $250-300.

French flared-rim water pitcher and matching basin, white with blue shading and a floral design. *Courtesy of Pam DeBisschop.* $300-400.

Small European coffee pot with hinged lid, 5" tall, green shading with red trim and a scenic design. *Courtesy of David T. Pikul, The Chuctanunda Antique Co.* $300-350.

French coffee biggin, 10" tall, blue with a daisy design. *Courtesy of David T. Pikul, The Chuctanunda Antique Co.* $400-500.

Early French bucket, 15" tall, rare piece with a detailed floral design on a white background. Note the design on lid. *Courtesy of David T. Pikul, The Chuctanunda Antique Co.* $850-1000.

French bucket from previous photo with a close-up depicting the riveted "ear" for attaching the handle. This detail indicates nineteenth century construction.

European coffee pot, 5" tall, unusual shape/handle/lid, white with a petite floral design. *Courtesy of David T. Pikul, The Chuctanunda Antique Co.* $325-400.

Early French chocolate pot with wooden handle, blue with a raised floral design. *Courtesy of David T. Pikul, The Chuctanunda Antique Co.* $500-600.

French coffee pot, 9" tall, white with a floral design and red trim. *Courtesy of David T. Pikul, The Chuctanunda Antique Co.* $300-350.

European coffee pot, 9" tall, light blue with red trim and a floral design. *Courtesy of David T. Pikul, The Chuctanunda Antique Co.* $275-350.

A pair of framed European stove plates, 7 1/2" wide by 17" long, blue with gilt trim and a raised floral design. *Courtesy of Ellen M. Plante.* $500-600 for the pair. Photo by Ted Plante.

French utensil rack, 12" wide by 19" long, white with pink shading, blue trim on drip basin, and a wildflower design. *Courtesy of David T. Pikul, The Chuctanunda Antique Co.* $275- 300.

Early French chocolate pot and bowl with handles/lid, white with blue bird motif. *Courtesy of David T. Pikul, The Chuctanunda Antique Co.* Chocolate pot $400-500 and bowl $350-400.

French wall-hung triple soap set for laundry, 15" wide, white with a floral design and French lettering. *Courtesy of David T. Pikul, The Chuctanunda Antique Co.* $400-500.

Large French coffee biggin, 14" tall, double handles, brown with pink roses. *Courtesy of David T. Pikul, The Chuctanunda Antique Co.* $400-500.

French chamber pail or bucket, 12" tall, white with a floral design. *Courtesy of David T. Pikul, The Chuctanunda Antique Co.* $400-450.

Round European bread box, metal handle and hinge, white with a rose design. *Courtesy of David T. Pikul, The Chuctanunda Antique Co.* $400-450.

European coffee pot, 9" tall, red with yellow striping and a daisy design. *Courtesy of David T. Pikul, The Chuctanunda Antique Co.* $250-300.

French foot bath, oval shape, 17 1/2" wide by 7" tall, white with a floral design. *Courtesy of Pam DeBisschop.* $500-600.

French coffee biggin, mid section removed to illustrate form, white with a hand-painted floral design. *Courtesy of David T. Pikul, The Chuctanunda Antique Co.* $375-450.

142

European trivet, 8" size, white with a red stencil design. *Courtesy of David T. Pikul, The Chuctanunda Antique Co.* $75-95.

French wall-hung utensil rack with two matching tools, 12" wide by 19" long, white with rare yellow shading and a wildflower design. *Courtesy of David T. Pikul, The Chuctanunda Antique Co.* $400-500.

French coffee biggin, 10 1/2" tall, light blue with a daisy design. *Courtesy of David T. Pikul, The Chuctanunda Antique Co.* $350-425.

French wall-hung match box, 7" tall, white with a floral design and French lettering. *Courtesy of David T. Pikul, The Chuctanunda Antique Co.* $250-300.

European body pitcher, 15" tall, white and blue shading with a sailboat design. *Courtesy of Ellen M. Plante.* $275-325. Photo by Ted Plante.

Large French coffee biggin, 14" tall, double handles, white with blue trim and a floral design. *Courtesy of David T. Pikul, The Chuctanunda Antique Co.* $400-500.

Two French memo boards, 12" and 9" tall, cream with floral designs. *Courtesy of David T. Pikul, The Chuctanunda Antique Co.* $275-350 each.

French pitcher, 7" tall, white with a pansy design. *Courtesy of David T. Pikul, The Chuctanunda Antique Co.* $275-325.

European coffee biggin, 10 1/2" tall, green with a white stripe and daisy motif. *Courtesy of David T. Pikul, The Chuctanunda Antique Co.* $400-500.

European coffee pot, 9" tall, white and light blue shading with a floral design. *Courtesy of David T. Pikul, The Chuctanunda Antique Co.* $250-300.

Small French measuring pitcher, 6" tall, brown with a floral design. *Courtesy of David T. Pikul, The Chuctanunda Antique Co.* $300-350.

145

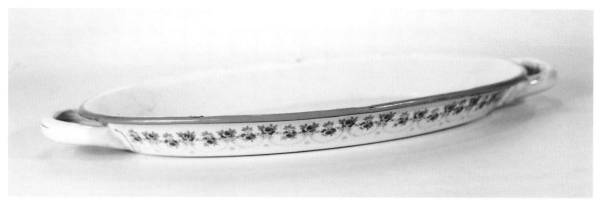

French tray, 14" long, white with blue trim and a petite garland of roses.
Courtesy of David T. Pikul, The Chuctanunda Antique Co. $165-200.

German utensil rack with single tool, white with cobalt trim, German lettering, and floral design. *Courtesy of David T. Pikul, The Chuctanunda Antique Co.* $400-500.

French body pitcher, 15" tall, white with red trim and a floral design. *Courtesy of David T. Pikul, The Chuctanunda Antique Co.* $300-375.

European chocolate pot, 6" tall, white with blue shading and a rose design. *Courtesy of David T. Pikul, The Chuctanunda Antique Co.* $300-400.

French umbrella stand, 19" tall, white with a floral design. *Courtesy of Pam DeBisschop.* $400-500.

European irrigator, rare cobalt blue with a bird/floral design. *Courtesy of David T. Pikul, The Chuctanunda Antique Co.* $375-450.

Round European bread box, metal handle and hinge, white with a blue floral design. *Courtesy of David T. Pikul, The Chuctanunda Antique Co.* $350-425.

French coffee pot, 9 1/2" tall, white with gilt trim and a large daisy/ leaf design. *Courtesy of David T. Pikul, The Chuctanunda Antique Co.* $350-400.

French water pitcher and matching basin, white with pink shading and a floral design. *Courtesy of David T. Pikul, The Chuctanunda Antique Co.* $600-700.

Ornate French coffee pot, 9" tall, featuring a rare floral design. *Courtesy of David T. Pikul, The Chuctanunda Antique Co.* $400-500.

German potato bucket, white with a scenic design. *Courtesy of David T. Pikul, The Chuctanunda Antique Co.* $275-350.

Large French coffee biggin, 14" tall, double handles, white with pink shading and a wildflower design. $400-500.

French coffee pot, 9" tall, light blue with a large floral design. *Courtesy of David T. Pikul, The Chuctanunda Antique Co.* $350-400.

American coffee pot with a wooden handle and metal lid, 10" tall, white with pink shading and a bird/floral motif. *Courtesy of David T. Pikul, The Chuctanunda Antique Co.* $300-350.

Late nineteenth century French lavabo with water dispenser and basin, brown with a bird/floral motif. *Courtesy of David T. Pikul, The Chuctanunda Antique Co.* $800-1000.

European coffee pot, 9" tall, light blue with a butterfly/floral motif. *Courtesy of David T. Pikul, The Chuctanunda Antique Co.* $350-400.

European teapot, pitcher, and mug, white with a rose design.
Courtesy of David T. Pikul, The Chuctanunda Antique Co. Teapot
$200-250, pitcher $200-225, and mug $75-100.

French coffee pot, 10" tall, white with a floral spray design.
Courtesy of David T. Pikul, The Chuctanunda Antique Co.
$400-500.

French chamber pail or bucket, 10" tall, unusual counter-weighted
disc in the lid which covers hole to contain odors, all-over blue
floral design. *Courtesy of David T. Pikul,
The Chuctanunda Antique Co.* $400-500.

French coffee biggin, 10 1/2" tall, medium blue with gilt trim and a petite floral design. *Courtesy of David T. Pikul, The Chuctanunda Antique Co.* $350-400.

French body pitcher, 15" tall, light blue with a bird/flower motif. *Courtesy of David T. Pikul, The Chuctanunda Antique Co.* $350-400.

French wall-hung salt box with wooden lid, 10" tall, white with blue shading, floral design, and French lettering. *Courtesy of David T. Pikul, The Chuctanunda Antique Co.* $250-325.

European casserole dish with lid, 10" diameter, white with blue stripes and a petite garland of roses. *Courtesy of David T. Pikul, The Chuctanunda Antique Co.* $275-300.

French coffee biggin, 10 1/2" tall, white with blue-green shading and a pansy design. *Courtesy of David T. Pikul, The Chuctanunda Antique Co.* $350-400.

European teapot, 5" tall, cobalt blue with a raised floral design and gilt trim. *Courtesy of David T. Pikul, The Chuctanunda Antique Co.* $350-400.

Late nineteenth century French coffee biggin, 10 1/2" tall, rare green with a stylized floral design. *Courtesy of David T. Pikul, The Chuctanunda Antique Co.* $375-450. Photo by Sarah Pikul.

153

French wall-hung triple soap for laundry, 15" wide, white with red trim, a floral motif, and French lettering. *Courtesy of David T. Pikul, The Chuctanunda Antique Co.* $300-400.

French spittoon, 9" diameter, white with pink trim and floral motif. *Courtesy of David T. Pikul, The Chuctanunda Antique Co.* $200-250.

European double lunch pail, white with a blue floral design. Note the riveted silverware holder below the handle. *Courtesy of David T. Pikul, The Chuctanunda Antique Co.* $300-350.

European wall-hung utensil rack with a single tool, 14" wide by 19" long, white with a red and green floral design. *Courtesy of David T. Pikul, The Chuctanunda Antique Co.* $400-450.

French coffee biggin, 10 1/2" tall, light blue with a floral design. *Courtesy of David T. Pikul, The Chuctanunda Antique Co.* $300-400.

French footbath, 17 1/2" wide by 7 1/2" tall, white with a rose design. *Courtesy of David T. Pikul, The Chuctanunda Antique Co.* $500-600.

Two-piece Czechoslovakian coffee set, blue with a floral pattern and white lettering. *Courtesy of David T. Pikul, The Chuctanunda Antique Co.* $300-400 for the pair.

French water pitcher with an all-over petite blue floral design. *Courtesy of Pam DeBisschop.* $275-325.

European coffee pot, 10" tall, brown with a scenic medallion surrounded by a leaf design. *Courtesy of David T. Pikul, The Chuctanunda Antique Co.* $325-375.

European coffee biggin, 10 1/2" tall, white with blue shading and a rose design. *Courtesy of David T. Pikul, The Chuctanunda Antique Co.* $300-400.

European coffee pot, 10" tall, blue with gilt trim and a raised bird/floral design. *Courtesy of David T. Pikul, The Chuctanunda Antique Co.* $325-365.

Large French coffee biggin, 14" tall, double handles, white with blue shading and a floral design. *Courtesy of David T. Pikul, The Chuctanunda Antique Co.* $500-600.

Rare French coffee grinder made during the late nineteenth century, white with a blue floral design. *Courtesy of David T. Pikul, The Chuctanunda Antique Co.* $600-800.

European coffee biggin, 10" tall, light blue with a darker blue and white floral motif. *Courtesy of David T. Pikul, The Chuctanunda Antique Co.* $250-300.

French body pitcher, 15" tall, white with blue shading, gilt trim, and a floral spray. *Courtesy of David T. Pikul, The Chuctanunda Antique Co.* $300-350.

Nineteenth century French pitcher, 12" tall, white with an ornate floral bouquet. *Courtesy of David T. Pikul, The Chuctanunda Antique Co.* $250-300.

French wall-hung match box, 7" tall, white with a petite garland of roses and French lettering. *Courtesy of David T. Pikul, The Chuctanunda Antique Co.* $250-300.

French coffee pot, pale yellow with gilt trim and a floral design. *Courtesy of Pam DeBisschop.* $375-450.

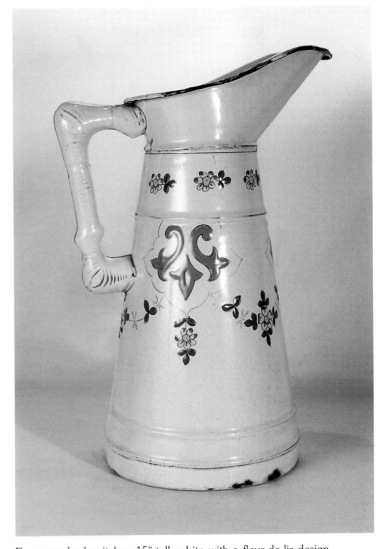

European teapot, 4" tall, red and white stripes combined with a garland of roses. *Courtesy of David T. Pikul, The Chuctanunda Antique Co.* $300-350.

European body pitcher, 15" tall, white with a fleur-de-lis design and petite flowers. Note the unusual handle which resembles decorative ceramics of the late nineteenth century era. *Courtesy of David T. Pikul, The Chuctanunda Antique Co.* $350-400.

Large French coffee biggin, 14" tall, double handles, white with blue shading and a wildflower design. *Courtesy of David T. Pikul, The Chuctanunda Antique Co.* $500-600.

French tear-drop shaped lavabo with a scalloped basin and matching soap dish, white with gilt trim and petite floral sprays. *Courtesy of David T. Pikul, The Chuctanunda Antique Co.* $800-1000.

European coffee biggin, 10 1/2" tall, brown shading and a white floral design. *Courtesy of David T. Pikul, The Chuctanunda Antique Co.* $350-425.

European coffee pot, 9" tall, white with blue shading and a rose motif. *Courtesy of David T. Pikul, The Chuctanunda Antique Co.* $250-300.

Late nineteenth century French body pitcher with hinged lid, 15" tall, white with a pink stylized design. *Courtesy of David T. Pikul, The Chuctanunda Antique Co.* $600-800.

French coffee biggin, 12" tall, double handles, white with a bird/floral motif. *Courtesy of David T. Pikul, The Chuctanunda Antique Co.* $500-600.

French colander, white with blue shading and a floral design. *Courtesy of David T. Pikul, The Chuctanunda Antique Co.* $250-300.

French teapot with a hinged lid, 5" tall, white with blue shading, gilt trim, and floral design. *Courtesy of David T. Pikul, The Chuctanunda Antique Co.* $250-275.

French coffee biggin, 10 1/2" tall, blue with a floral spray. *Courtesy of David T. Pikul, The Chuctanunda Antique Co.* $400-500.

French measuring pitcher, 9" tall, brown shading with a white floral spray. *Courtesy of David T. Pikul, The Chuctanunda Antique Co.* $250-300.

French five-piece canister set, white with French lettering and a garland of roses design. *Courtesy of David T. Pikul, The Chuctanunda Antique Co.* $500-600.

French chocolate pot, 10" tall, hinged lid and wooden handle, white with a floral design. *Courtesy of David T. Pikul, The Chuctanunda Antique Co.* $400-450.

French coffee biggin, 10 1/2" tall, blue with a floral design. *Courtesy of David T. Pikul, The Chuctanunda Antique Co.* $400-500. Photo by Sarah Pikul.

Early French measuring pitcher, 9" tall, pale blue with a red rim and bird design. *Courtesy of David T. Pikul, The Chuctanunda Antique Co.* $300-350.

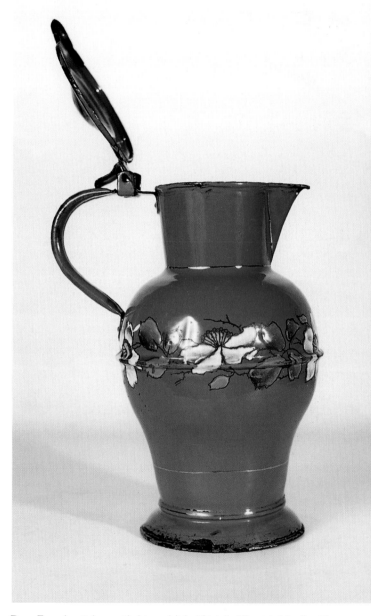

Rare French pitcher with hinged lid, 10" tall, "French blue" with a floral design. *Courtesy of David T. Pikul, The Chuctanunda Antique Co.* $400-500.

European coffee pot, 6" tall, cobalt blue with a daisy design. *Courtesy of David T. Pikul, The Chuctanunda Antique Co.* $125-175.

European teapot, 3 1/2" tall, light blue with a raised floral design. *Courtesy of David T. Pikul, The Chuctanunda Antique Co.* $400-500.

French coffee biggin, 10" tall, white with pale blue shading, cobalt trim, and a wildflower design. *Courtesy of David T. Pikul, The Chuctanunda Antique Co.* $350-400.

French body pitcher, 15" tall, blue with a rose design. *Courtesy of David T. Pikul, The Chuctanunda Antique Co.* $300-400.

French cache pot, 9" tall, white with pink shading and a floral spray. *Courtesy of David T. Pikul, The Chuctanunda Antique Co.* $350-400.

French utensil rack, 14" wide by 19" long, rare combination of a blue mottled pattern and a floral design. *Courtesy of David T. Pikul, The Chuctanunda Antique Co.* $350-400.

Large French coffee biggin, 14" tall, double handles, apple green with a cherry design. *Courtesy of David T. Pikul, The Chuctanunda Antique Co.* $350-400. Photo by Sarah Pikul.

European wall-hung brush bin, white with a blue stylized design. *Courtesy of David T. Pikul, The Chuctanunda Antique Co.* $200-250.

European coffee biggin, 10 1/2" tall, white with a petite band of flowers. *Courtesy of David T. Pikul, The Chuctanunda Antique Co.* $300-400.

Large French coffee biggin, 14" tall, double handles, white with gilt trim and a daisy design. *Courtesy of David T. Pikul, The Chuctanunda Antique Co.* $400-500.

French tear-drop shaped lavabo, white with blue shading and a floral design. *Courtesy of David T. Pikul, The Chuctanunda Antique Co.* $600-700.

French coffee biggin, 10 1/2" tall, rare yellow shading and floral spray. *Courtesy of David T. Pikul, The Chuctanunda Antique Co.* $600-700.

French utensil rack with two tools, 12" wide by 19" long, white with blue shading and a floral motif. *Courtesy of David T. Pikul, The Chuctanunda Antique Co.* $300-400.

European umbrella stand, 19" tall, white with blue shading and gilt trim, hand-painted parrot and tulips. *Courtesy of Ellen M. Plante.* $700-800. Photo by Ted Plante.

French coffee biggin, 10 1/2" tall, pale blue with a floral design. *Courtesy of David T. Pikul, The Chuctanunda Antique Co.* $375-425.

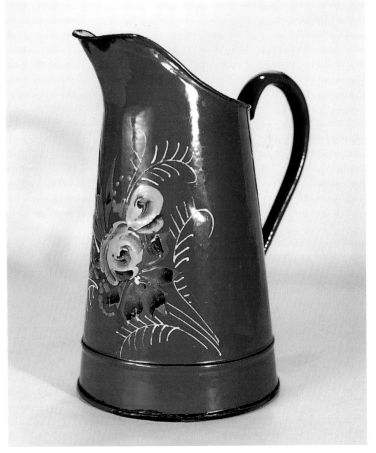

French measuring pitcher, 9 1/2" tall, blue with roses. *Courtesy of David T. Pikul, The Chuctanunda Antique Co.* $300-400.

Matching European body pitcher and chamber pail with lid, cream with a "French blue" floral design and trim. *Courtesy of David T. Pikul, The Chuctanunda Antique Co.* $500-600 for the set.

Large French coffee biggin, 14" tall, double handles, white with gilt trim and a bird/floral design. *Courtesy of David T. Pikul, The Chuctanunda Antique Co.* $600-750.

French coffee biggin, 10" tall, light blue with a raised bird and flower design. *Courtesy of David T. Pikul, The Chuctanunda Antique Co.* $600-700.

European covered soap dish, 5" diameter, white with blue shading and a rose design. *Courtesy of David T. Pikul, The Chuctanunda Antique Co.* $175-225.

French coffee biggin, rare pale green color with a floral design. *Courtesy of David T. Pikul, The Chuctanunda Antique Co.* $400-500.

European coffee biggin, 12" tall, double handles, brown with a white floral design. *Courtesy of David T. Pikul, The Chuctanunda Antique Co.* $400-500.

French body pitcher, 15" tall, white with blue shading and roses. *Courtesy of David T. Pikul, The Chuctanunda Antique Co.* $350-425.

French coffee biggin, 10" tall, red with air-brushed floral design. As the next few photos illustrate it is indeed possible to build a collection based on a favorite color or design. *Courtesy of David T. Pikul, The Chuctanunda Antique Co.* $300-400.

French four-piece canister set and matching wall-hung salt box. *Courtesy of David T. Pikul, The Chuctanunda Antique Co.* Canisters $350-400 and the salt box $200-250.

Assorted pitchers ranging in size from 6" to 10" tall. *Courtesy of David T. Pikul, The Chuctanunda Antique Co.* $250-300 each.

Matching lavabo and body pitcher. *Courtesy of David T. Pikul, The Chuctanunda Antique Co.* Lavabo $450-500 and the pitcher $275-325.

French wall-hung utensil rack with the same air-brushed/stenciled floral design. *Courtesy of David T. Pikul, The Chuctanunda Antique Co.* $300-350.

French milk pail, 9" tall, white with a wildflower design. *Courtesy of David T. Pikul, The Chuctanunda Antique Co.* $225-250.

Large French coffee biggin, 14" tall, double handles, white with a blue rim and rose design. *Courtesy of David T. Pikul, The Chuctanunda Antique Co.* $350-425.

Large French coffee biggin, 14" tall, double handles, white with blue-green shading and a floral spray. *Courtesy of David T. Pikul, The Chuctanunda Antique Co.* $400-500.

American teapot, white and blue shading with a floral design and metal trim. *Courtesy of David T. Pikul, The Chuctanunda Antique Co.* $400-500.

Large European coffee biggin, 14" tall, double handles, white with green shading and a floral/nature design. *Courtesy of David T. Pikul, The Chuctanunda Antique Co.* $300-400.

French teapot, 4" tall, white with gilt trim and a daisy design. *Courtesy of David T. Pikul, The Chuctanunda Antique Co.* $300-400.

French body pitcher, 15" tall, blue with a rose design. *Courtesy of David T. Pikul, The Chuctanunda Antique Co.* $350-400.

Additional Reading

Books

Bishop, Christina. *Miller's Collecting Kitchenware.* London, England: Miller's (an imprint of Reed Books), 1995.

Greguire, Helen. *The Collector's Encyclopedia of Granite Ware.* Paducah, Kentucky: Collector Books, 1990.

Greguire, Helen. *The Collector's Encyclopedia of Granite Ware Book II.* Paducah, Kentucky: Collector Books, 1993.

Lifshey, Earl. *The Housewares Story.* Chicago, Illinois: National Housewares Manufacturers Association, 1973.

Pikul, David and Ellen M. Plante. *Collectible Enameled Ware: American & European.* Atglen, Pennsylvania: Schiffer Publishing, Ltd., 1998.

Plante, Ellen M. *The American Kitchen 1700 to the Present.* New York, New York:Facts On File, Inc., 1995.

Vogelzang, Vernagene and Evelyn Welch. *Graniteware: Collector's Guide with Prices.* Lombard, Illinois: Wallace-Homestead Book Company, 1981.

Vogelzang, Vernagene and Evelyn Welch. *Granite Ware: Collector's Guide with Prices Book II.* Radnor, Pennsylvania, 1986.

Von Eicken, Brigitte ten Kate. *L'ÉMail dans la maison.* Paris, France: Armand Colin, 1992.

Periodicals

Cabré, Monique, "A La Cuisine - les ustensiles créent," *Aladin*, March 1999: 27.

"Enamelware Coffeepots," *Country Living*, February 1999: 88.

"French Enamelware," *Country Living*, February 1997: 76.

Johnson, Julia Claiborne, "Enamelware," *Martha Stewart Living*, June/July 1994: 35.

Masclaux-Perron, Anne-Marie, "La Tôle Emaillee," *Maison et Décors Méditérraine*, Dec 96/Jan 97: 18

Plante, Ellen M., "Enamel Imports - Old-World Kitchen Collectibles," *Country Collectibles*, Fall 1995: 32.

Plante, Ellen M., "Hold Everything," *Country Living*, June 1997: 80.

"Tôlèperpétuité," *Art & Decoration*, Jan/Feb. 1999: 106.

Weiss, Gloria K., "Graniteware," *Country Living*, November 1996: 20.